YORK NOTES

BLOOD BROTHERS

WILLY RUSSELL

NOTES BY DAVID GRANT

PEARSON

y **YORK PRESS**

YORK PRESS
322 Old Brompton Road, London SW5 9JH

PEARSON EDUCATION LIMITED
Edinburgh Gate, Harlow,
Essex CM20 2JE, United Kingdom

Associated companies, branches and representatives throughout the world

First published 2016

10 9 8 7 6 5 4 3 2 1

ISBN 978–1–2921–3806–0

Illustrations by Tony O'Donnell; and Moreno Chiacchiera (page 61 only)
Phototypeset by DTP Media

Photo credits: Jeabsam/Shutterstock for page 8 / Grigorenko/Thinkstock for
page 9 / © iStock/AGouldDesign for page 11 top / © iStock/CherriesJD
for page 11 bottom / © iStock/Dominik Pabis for page 12 /
© iStock/169alexandermendoza for page 13 / carlatayler/Shutterstock for
page 14 / © iStock/SolStock for page 15 / mpalis/Thinkstock for page 16
/ © iStock/bbbrrn for page 18 / © iStock/frankwright for page 19 / Dani
Simmonds/Shutterstock for page 22 / © iStock/Vintervit for page 25 top /
Rosa Jay/Shutterstock for page 25 bottom / edwardolive/Shutterstock for
page 27 / © iStock/George Clerk for page 29 / © iStock/JohnGollop for page
31 / Dan Kospayer/Shutterstock for page 35 / © iStock/jessekarjalainen for
page 36 / © iStock/Scukrov for page 37 / AndrijTer/Thinkstock for page 39 /
© iStock/ImagineGolf for page 41 / © iStock/vandervelden for page 51 top
/ © iStock/Studio-Annika for page 51 bottom / © iStock/Difydave for page
53 top / Willowisp/Thinkstock for page 53 bottom / © iStock/ianlangley
for page 54 / pasmal/amanaimagesRF/Thinkstock for page 55 / © iStock/
Wendelland Carolyn for page 57 / Dave M Bennett/Getty for page 58 top/
B Christopher/Alamy for page 58 bottom / David Cole/Alamy for page 59
top / © iStock/Rpsycho for page 59 bottom / s_white/Thinkstock for page 60
/ © iStock/chapin31 for page 63 / © iStock/Chris Hepburn for page 64 /
© iStock/Jasmina007 for page 67 bottom / © iStock/rafal_olechowski for
page 68 / yavuzunlu/Shutterstock for page 70

CONTENTS

PART FOUR:
THEMES, CONTEXTS AND SETTINGS

PART FIVE:
FORM, STRUCTURE AND LANGUAGE

PART SIX:
PROGRESS BOOSTER ★

PART SEVEN:
FURTHER STUDY AND ANSWERS

PREPARING FOR ASSESSMENT

HOW WILL I BE ASSESSED ON MY WORK ON *BLOOD BROTHERS*?

All exam boards are different, but whichever course you are following, your work will be examined through at least three of these four Assessment Objectives:

Assessment Objectives	Wording	Worth thinking about ...
AO1	Read, understand and respond to texts. Students should be able to: ● maintain a critical style and develop an informed personal response ● use textual references, including quotations, to support and illustrate interpretations.	● How well do I know what happens, what people say, do, etc.? ● What do I think about the key ideas in the play? ● How can I support my viewpoint in a really convincing way? ● What are the best quotations to use and when should I use them?
AO2 *	Analyse the language, form and structure used by a writer to create meanings and effects, using relevant subject terminology where appropriate.	● What specific things does the writer 'do'? What choices has Russell made (why this particular word, phrase or speech here? Why does this event happen at this point?) ● What effects do these choices create – suspense? Sympathy? Horror?
AO3 *	Show understanding of the relationships between texts and the contexts in which they were written.	● What can I learn about society from the play? (What does it tell me about family and class, for example?) ● What was society like at the time in which the play is set? Can I see it reflected in the text?
AO4	Use a range of vocabulary and sentence structures for clarity, purpose and effect, with accurate spelling and punctuation.	● How accurately and clearly do I write? ● Are there small errors of grammar, spelling and punctuation I can get rid of?

* For *Blood Brothers*, AO2 is not examined by Edexcel; AO3 is not examined by Eduqas

Look out for the Assessment Objective labels throughout your York Notes Study Guide – these will help to focus your study and revision!

The text used in these Notes is the Bloomsbury, Methuen Drama Modern Classics edition, 2001 (reissued 2009).

HOW TO USE YOUR YORK NOTES STUDY GUIDE

You are probably wondering what is the best and most efficient way to use your York Notes Study Guide on *Blood Brothers*. Here are three possibilities:

A **step-by-step** study and revision guide	A **'dip-in' support** when you need it	A **revision guide** after you have finished the text
Step 1: Read Part Two as you read the text, as a companion to help you study it. **Step 2:** When you need to, turn to Parts Three to Five to focus your learning. **Step 3:** Then, when you have finished, use Parts Six and Seven to hone your exam skills, revise and practise for the exam.	Perhaps you know the text quite well, but you want to check your understanding and practise your exam skills? Just look for the section you think you need most help with and go for it!	You might want to use the Notes after you have finished your study, using Parts Two to Five to check over what you have learned, and then work through Parts Six and Seven in the weeks leading up to your exam.

HOW WILL THE GUIDE HELP YOU STUDY AND REVISE?

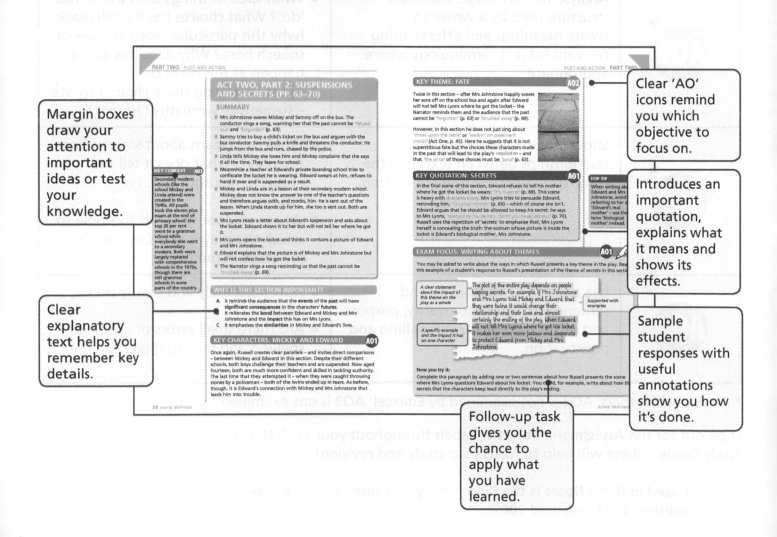

Margin boxes draw your attention to important ideas or test your knowledge.

Clear explanatory text helps you remember key details.

Clear **'AO'** icons remind you which objective to focus on.

Introduces an important quotation, explains what it means and shows its effects.

Sample student responses with useful annotations show you how it's done.

Follow-up task gives you the chance to apply what you have learned.

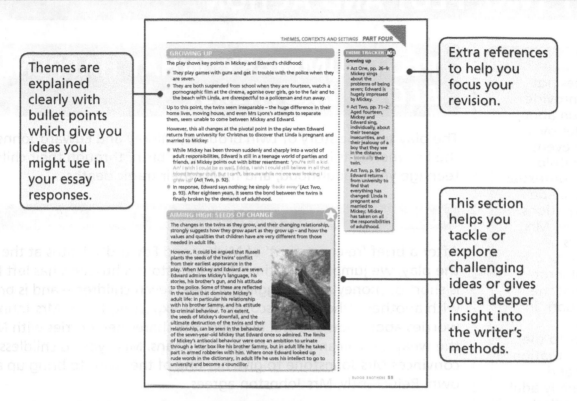

Themes are explained clearly with bullet points which give you ideas you might use in your essay responses.

Extra references to help you focus your revision.

This section helps you tackle or explore challenging ideas or gives you a deeper insight into the writer's methods.

Parts Two to Five end with a **Progress and Revision Check**:

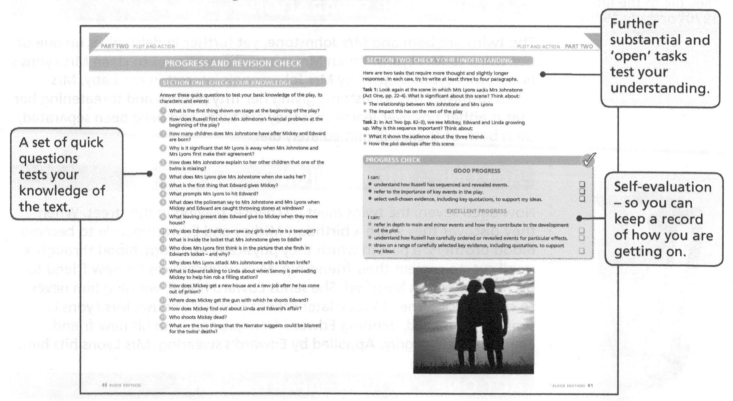

A set of quick questions tests your knowledge of the text.

Further substantial and 'open' tasks test your understanding.

Self-evaluation – so you can keep a record of how you are getting on.

Don't forget Parts Six and Seven, with advice and practice on **improving your writing skills**:

● Focus on **difficult areas** such as **'context'** and **'inferences'**

● **Short snippets** of **other students' work** to show you how it's done (or not done!)

● Three annotated **sample responses** to a task **at different levels**, with **expert comments**, to help you judge your own level

● **Practice questions**

● **Answers** to the **Progress and Revision Checks** and **Checkpoint** margin boxes

Now it's up to you! Don't forget – there's even more help on our website with more sample answers, essay planners and even online tutorials. Go to www.yorknotes.com to find out more.

KEY CONTEXT (A03)

Russell does not explicitly provide information about the decades over which the events of the play unfold. However, contextual clues do provide some suggestions. For example, Mrs Johnstone's references to Marilyn Monroe suggest that the twins are born in the 1950s. References to the economic situation in Mickey and Edward's early adult life suggest that they die in the late 1970s or early 1980s.

PLOT SUMMARY: WHAT HAPPENS IN *BLOOD BROTHERS*?

The play tells the story of twin brothers, Mickey and Edward Johnstone, via the key moments in their lives: from their birth, through their childhood, teenage years, adulthood, and finally their tragic deaths.

ACT ONE – THE TWINS ARE ON THEIR WAY

After a brief 're-enactment' of Mickey and Edward's deaths at the end of the play, we jump back in time. Mrs Johnstone's husband has left her. She is short of money and struggling to feed seven children – and is pregnant with another. When she discovers she is expecting twins, Mrs Johnstone worries about how she will manage. She shares her worries with Mrs Lyons, the wealthy woman whose house she cleans. Mrs Lyons is childless and convinces Mrs Johnstone to give her one of the twins to bring up as her own. Reluctantly, Mrs Johnston agrees.

ACT ONE – THE SEPARATION

The twins are born and Mrs Johnstone, yet further in debt, gives up one of her twins to Mrs Lyons. When Mrs Johnstone next goes to clean Mrs Lyons's house, Mrs Lyons is upset by Mrs Johnstone's interest in her baby. Mrs Lyons dismisses Mrs Johnstone, giving her fifty pounds and threatening her that if either boy ever learns that they are twins and have been separated, then both of them will immediately die.

ACT ONE – THE REUNION

Now aged seven, the twins meet by chance, playing in the street. When they discover they share a birthday, Mickey and Edward decide to become blood brothers: a pact in which they physically exchange blood through a small cut, to cement their friendship. Mickey introduces his new friend to his mother who is horrified. She sends Edward home, warning him never to come back. When Mickey later calls at Edward's house, Mrs Lyons is similarly dismayed, banning Edward from playing with his new friend. Edward reacts angrily. Appalled by Edward's swearing, Mrs Lyons hits him.

ACT ONE – MOVING APART AGAIN

Mickey, his older brother Sammy and his friend Linda play while Edward looks on, bored and alone. Mickey tempts Edward out to play and Mrs Lyons panics at his disappearance. A policeman catches Edward, Mickey and Linda throwing stones at windows. The policeman threatens Mrs Johnstone with a court appearance – and warns Mrs Lyons that her son should be kept away from children like Mickey. Mr and Mrs Lyons decide to move house. Edward goes to say goodbye to Mrs Johnstone. She gives him a locket containing a picture of her and Mickey, warning him to keep it hidden. She decides she too will move to a new house and a bright new future.

ACT TWO – THE TWINS LEAD PARALLEL LIVES

The Johnstones and the Lyons are in their new homes. The twins, now fourteen, seem to lead very different lives: Edward is returning to his boarding school while Mickey gets the bus to the local school. However, the twins are not so different: Edward is suspended from school for refusing to give up his locket and swearing at a teacher; Mickey and Linda are suspended for challenging their teacher. Edward shows his mother the locket. She is shocked when she sees the picture inside.

ACT TWO – THE TWINS GROW UP TOGETHER

Mickey and Edward are reunited by chance. Mickey is struggling to express his feelings for Linda and the boys decide that watching *Nymphomaniac Nights* and *Swedish Au Pairs* at the cinema may help. Mrs Lyons follows them to Mrs Johnstone's house. Seemingly mentally disturbed, she confronts Mrs Johnstone, first offering her money to move away, then threatening her with a knife. Mrs Johnstone sends her away.

Mickey, Edward and Linda spend their teenage years together. Mickey leaves school and works in a job he hates. Edward goes to university. Mickey has still not revealed his true feelings to Linda while Edward has been concealing his feelings for her. With Edward's encouragement, Mickey finally tells Linda how he feels.

ACT TWO – THE TWINS GROW APART

Linda is pregnant. Mickey marries her and then finds he has been made redundant. Edward returns from university for Christmas. The twins seem to have grown further apart. While Sammy persuades Mickey to be a lookout in a robbery he is planning, Edward declares his love for Linda and proposes. Linda tells him she has married Mickey and is pregnant.

ACT TWO – THE CLIMAX

Mickey is arrested and imprisoned for his part in the robbery. Released from prison and taking medication for depression, Mickey comes home to a new house and a new job – which he guesses was arranged by Edward who is now a local councillor. Linda begins an affair with Edward. Mickey sees them together, takes his brother's gun to a council meeting intending to shoot Edward but cannot bring himself to do it. His mother reveals the truth: they are twins. In shock, Mickey pulls the trigger by mistake and kills Edward. The police shoot Mickey dead.

REVISION FOCUS: MAKE SURE YOU KNOW WHAT HAPPENS

Use a timeline to plot the key events in the play in chronological order. Highlight the key turning points: the events which most clearly show how and why Mickey and Edward's relationship develops and changes. Note the Act and page on which each significant event occurs.

> **CHECKPOINT 1** (A02)
>
> When do Mickey's and Edward's lives seem most similar? When do they seem most different?

> **TOP TIP** (A02)
>
> Remember: *Blood Brothers* is not just a story or a script; it is a play, written for live performance. So you need to think about how it could be performed on stage, and the impact the staging might have on an audience.

TOP TIP (A02)

Think about the Narrator as a dramatic device – a character created by Russell to tell the story and manipulate the audience's response to it.

CHECKPOINT 2 (A02)

Why do you think Russell chooses a milkman to highlight Mrs Johnstone's financial difficulties?

ACT ONE, PART 1: THE STORY BEGINS (PP. 5–8)

SUMMARY

- The Narrator reveals the entire story of the Johnstone twins from birth to death.

- Mrs Johnstone describes, in song, the story of her marriage: how her husband flattered her, married her when they discovered she was pregnant, and finally left her with seven children and another on the way.

- The Milkman complains that Mrs Johnstone's payment for milk deliveries is overdue. Mrs Johnstone explains that she is pregnant and has a new job and that he will be paid soon, but the Milkman is unsympathetic.

- Mrs Johnstone's children all complain of hunger. She reassures them, listing all the delicious food they will have next week when she starts her new job.

WHY IS THIS SECTION IMPORTANT?

A   It **summarises** the **entire plot** of the play, revealing the **inevitable fates** of its central characters.

B   It introduces **Mrs Johnstone** and the story of her **marriage**.

C   We learn that Mrs Johnstone has **no money** and is struggling to bring up **seven children**.

D   It highlights the importance of Mrs Johnstone's **new job** to the well-being of her **family**.

KEY QUOTATION: SYMPATHY FOR MRS JOHNSTONE (A02)

The Narrator introduces Mrs Johnstone, saying: 'An' did y' never hear of the mother, so cruel, / There's a stone in place of her heart?' (p. 5). Here Russell seems to be suggesting that society might jump to the conclusion that a mother who gives away a child must be cold and heartless. However, immediately after this, he focuses the scene on the circumstances that drove Mrs Johnstone to that decision and so maintains the audience's sympathy for her.

KEY STRUCTURE: THE PROLOGUE (A02)

The very first few lines of *Blood Brothers* are a kind of prologue, summarising the story of the play and revealing that the twins will both die. A reader's or an audience's interest is often sustained by wanting to find out how a story ends. However, the opening of *Blood Brothers* encourages the audience to ask how and why the twins will die, and to be aware throughout the play that their deaths will be the result of all the characters' choices and actions that we see on stage.

AIMING HIGH: COMMENTING ON MUSICAL FORM ⭐

Some musicals are described as 'sung through' – the story is entirely told through song and they contain no spoken dialogue at all. *Blood Brothers*, however, contains far more dialogue than song and so it is important to consider why and where the writer chooses to use song.

One way in which Russell uses song is to express a character's thoughts and feelings without the need for that character to reveal them to another character. In effect, the songs have the same function as a soliloquy. For example, in this section, Mrs Johnstone sings a song suggesting the romance with which her marriage began and her regret at the life of drudgery and financial difficulty in which it resulted.

The song does, however, end on a positive note as it returns when she sings to her children, reassuring them that they will soon have plenty to eat. Perhaps the events recounted in the first part of the song suggest that her hopes in the second part of the song will also end in disappointment.

KEY CONTEXT (A03)

Shakespeare uses a similar structural technique in both *Macbeth* and *Romeo and Juliet*, revealing the fates of the central characters at, or near, the start of the play. In *Romeo and Juliet*, Shakespeare uses a Chorus – similar to the Narrator in *Blood Brothers* – to do this.

KEY CONTEXT (A03)

Marilyn Monroe was an actress and model in the 1950s and 1960s. Mrs Johnstone's references to her in this section of the play suggest an ideal of beauty and glamour in ironic contrast to the reality of Mrs Johnstone's life. They also, perhaps, suggest the tragic end to which the play is moving: Marilyn Monroe died of a drugs overdose, presumed intentional, in 1963.

ACT ONE, PART 2: MRS JOHNSTONE AND MRS LYONS MAKE AN AGREEMENT (PP. 8–16)

SUMMARY

- Mrs Johnstone has started her new job as Mrs Lyons's cleaner.
- Mrs Lyons explains that her husband has been sent away on business for nine months, and reveals that she and her husband have not been able to have children.
- Mrs Johnstone is shocked when Mrs Lyons puts a pair of new shoes on her table as she considers it bad luck.
- The Gynaecologist informs Mrs Johnstone that she is expecting twins.
- Mrs Johnstone is worried that she will not cope with another two mouths to feed. She tells Mrs Lyons who suggests that Mrs Johnstone give her one of the twins to bring up as her own. As her husband is away, she can conceal the truth from him.
- Mrs Lyons suggests that the twins will be taken into care if Mrs Johnstone cannot look after them and points out what a good life the child would have with her.
- Satisfied that Mrs Lyons will let her see the child every day, Mrs Johnstone agrees to the plan. Mrs Lyons makes her swear to the agreement on a Bible.

WHY IS THIS SECTION IMPORTANT?

A   It **introduces** the character of **Mrs Lyons** and shows us her **relationship** with **Mrs Johnstone**.

B   It reveals the **agreement** between Mrs Johnstone and Mrs Lyons which begins the play's inevitable progression to **tragedy**.

C   It explains the **positive reasons** for Mrs Johnstone's decision to **give up** one of her **children**.

D   It introduces the theme of **superstition** which plays a significant part in some of Mrs Johnstone's decisions later in the play.

KEY CHARACTER: MRS LYONS   (A01)

In her first appearance in this section, Mrs Lyons is presented sympathetically: she lives in a house large enough for the children that she and her husband planned but could not have. She laughs, perhaps patronisingly, at Mrs Johnstone's superstition but agrees to remove her new shoes from the table 'if it will make you any happier' (p. 9).

Her desperation for children, and the lengths to which it will drive her, become more apparent in her second appearance when she learns that Mrs Johnstone is expecting twins and asks her to give her one of them. Faced with Mrs Johnstone's reluctance, her persuasion becomes more aggressive: she asks Mrs Johnstone how she can 'possibly avoid some of them being put into care' (p. 12) if she has two more children and then makes her swear to their agreement on the Bible. Although Mrs Johnstone agrees for the sake of the children, Russell strongly suggests that she has been manipulated by Mrs Lyons.

KEY LANGUAGE: CONTRASTING DIALOGUE (A02)

There are notable differences in the way in which Mrs Johnstone and Mrs Lyons speak.

Mrs Johnstone's speech is full of abbreviations, contractions and language choices suggesting her Liverpool dialect and accent: 'I was dead worried about havin' another baby ... I didn't see how we were gonna manage' (p. 10).

Mrs Lyons's speech is in standard English and is much more formal. She refers to 'children' while Mrs Johnstone talks about her 'kids'. Mrs Lyons reminds Mrs Johnstone that she is 'being threatened by the welfare people' (p. 12) whereas Mrs Johnstone says 'The welfare have already been on to me' (p. 11). Russell uses these differing language choices to reflect the difference in their social class.

KEY CHARACTER: THE NARRATOR (A01)

The traditional role of the narrator is to tell the story, explaining and linking the key moments as they are played out on stage. Russell's Narrator does fulfil this role – however he performs another equally significant function in this section and throughout the play: having revealed the twins' eventual death at the very start of the play, he constantly reminds the audience that each step that the characters take is another step towards their tragic end. In this way, Russell uses the Narrator to build tension throughout the play and emphasise the part that all the characters play in its resolution.

AIMING HIGH: THE ROLE OF SUPERSTITION ⭐

It is important that you can discuss the role of superstition in the play. In this section of Act One, Russell establishes Mrs Johnstone's belief in superstition when she is alarmed to find that Mrs Lyons has put new shoes on a table.

Russell highlights her belief and Mrs Lyons's disbelief as a significant difference between them. It perhaps suggests that superstition is more typical of the uneducated Mrs Johnstone, and is ridiculous to the more educated Mrs Lyons.

Later, when Mrs Lyons declares that the twins will die if they ever discover the truth, it implies that she is exploiting Mrs Johnstone's tendency to believe in superstitions in order to manipulate her.

More significantly, though, Russell uses Mrs Johnstone's belief as a plot device. It explains her reasons for not revealing the truth to the twins until the very end of the play. If revealed, their relationship as brothers would, of course, have a significant impact on their lives, on their actions and reactions, and on the course of the play.

KEY CONTEXT (A03)

The Narrator's function in *Blood Brothers* is similar to that of the Chorus in Ancient Greek drama. The Chorus was a body of ten or more actors who would recite their lines in unison, providing the audience with explanations of, and commentary on, the action on stage. Unlike the Narrator in *Blood Brothers*, they would not take on other roles and become involved directly in the action of the play.

ACT ONE, PART 3: THE TWINS ARE BORN AND SEPARATED (PP. 16–20)

SUMMARY

- The twins are born.
- Mrs Johnstone is confronted by various debt collectors. She owes money to them all.
- The debt collectors take goods from her house because she cannot pay them.
- Mrs Lyons comes to see Mrs Johnstone and discovers that the twins have been born. She reminds Mrs Johnstone of their agreement.
- Mrs Johnstone asks Mrs Lyons to choose one of the children. She does so and leaves with the child, telling Mrs Johnstone to take a week off work.
- Mrs Johnstone explains to her other children that the missing twin has gone to heaven.
- Hearing about the treats the missing twin will enjoy in heaven, Mrs Johnstone's other children demand their own treats from the catalogue.

WHY IS THIS SECTION IMPORTANT?

A The **separation** of the twins is a **pivotal** moment in the play. It begins a series of events which will inevitably end in **tragedy**.

B It shows some of the **reasons** for Mrs Johnstone's decision to give away her child: the **pressure** she is under from Mrs Lyons, her other children and her **financial situation**.

CHECKPOINT 4 (A02)

How does Russell make a connection in this section between the money that Mrs Johnstone owes the debt collectors and her agreement with Mrs Lyons?

KEY SETTINGS: CONTRASTING HOMES

In the production note on page 2 of the play, Russell provides some ideas for its staging, suggesting there should be 'no cumbersome scene changes'. Only two areas of the stage are 'semi-permanent': the Lyons house and the Johnstone house. The Lyons house is described as 'comfortable' and the Johnstone house is seen only from the outside. Their two houses are central to the action of the play and clearly reflect the characters who live in them.

Just before this section of Act One, the audience sees Mrs Lyons in her home. Mrs Johnstone describes the house as 'lovely', while Mrs Lyons thinks it is 'pretty' and 'large' (Act One, p. 8). Although the audience may not be shown the interior of Mrs Johnstone's home, its deprivation is strongly suggested in the arrival of the debt collectors and her children's demands for food and material possessions. In this section, the contrast between the two houses emphasises at least some of the reasons for Mrs Johnstone's decision to give up one of her twins, and suggests the difference in the lives the boys will lead.

KEY QUOTATION: THE TROUBLE WITH MRS JOHNSTONE

In this section of Act One, the Finance Man advises Mrs Johnstone that she should not buy things that she cannot afford. She replies: 'I know I shouldn't ... I've spent all me ... life knowin' I *shouldn't*. But I do.' (p. 17) This seems to suggest good intentions and a failure to carry them out in every aspect of her life: she knows she should control her money and her children, but seems unable to do either effectively. It suggests her failings are not a result of ignorance, but of her circumstances and, perhaps, her lack of self-discipline.

REVISION FOCUS: WHY DOES MRS JOHNSTONE GIVE ONE OF HER TWINS AWAY?

Giving away a child is clearly a desperate act. At the start of the play, the Narrator suggests that a mother who could do such a thing must have 'a stone in place of her heart' (Act One, p. 5). In a table, or in two columns, note down all the ways in which Willy Russell:

- maintains the audience's sympathy for Mrs Johnstone by encouraging them to understand why she gives away her child
- uses the Narrator and other characters to condemn Mrs Johnstone for giving away her child

KEY CONTEXT

It has been estimated that as many as 10 per cent of families in Britain lived in poverty in the 1950s.

ACT ONE, PART 4: MRS LYONS SACKS MRS JOHNSTONE (PP. 20–4)

SUMMARY

- As Mrs Johnstone and Mr and Mrs Lyons are looking at the new baby, Mrs Johnstone wants to pick him up, but Mrs Lyons tells her not to.
- Having persuaded her husband that they should sack Mrs Johnstone, Mrs Lyons dismisses her, giving her fifty pounds.
- Mrs Johnstone agrees to leave but says she will take the baby with her.
- Mrs Lyons threatens her with the police and the superstition that both twins will die if they ever learn that they were separated.
- Mrs Johnstone takes the money and leaves.
- The Narrator's song ominously suggests that disaster will soon follow.

WHY IS THIS SECTION IMPORTANT?

A This is the first appearance of **Mr Lyons**.
B **Mrs Lyons's character**, and the **audience's response** to her, is **developed** through her treatment of **Mrs Johnstone**.
C The **connection** between **Mrs Johnstone** and one of her twins seems to have been **permanently severed**.

KEY CHARACTER: MRS LYONS (A01)

Before this section, Russell establishes some sympathy for Mrs Lyons as she reveals that she and her husband hoped to have children but could not. This sympathy is soon undermined as she manipulatively persuades Mrs Johnstone to agree to give up her child. Now with each appearance of Mrs Lyons, Russell seems to be chipping away at any remaining sympathy for her.

In this section, Mrs Lyons deceives her husband as she explains why she wants to sack Mrs Johnstone. She then seeks to control Mrs Johnstone by making up the superstition that the twins will die if they learn that they were separated – which the audience already knows Mrs Johnstone is likely to believe. Her ruthlessness in dismissing Mrs Johnstone from her job – which the audience and Mrs Lyons know she relies on – strongly suggests how Russell intends the audience to respond to the play's two mothers: Mrs Lyons has become the villain of the play and Mrs Johnstone her helpless victim. It is only her desperation to have a child which, perhaps, excuses Mrs Lyons's actions in this section.

TOP TIP (A02)

There are always two sides to every story. None of Russell's characters are all good or all bad. Think about ways in which he tries to create both negative and positive responses to his characters – often at the same time.

KEY QUOTATION: 'YOU KNOW WHAT WILL HAPPEN' (A02)

When Mrs Lyons tells Mrs Johnstone about the superstition regarding separated twins, Russell's use of punctuation suggests that he intends the audience to recognise that she has invented it: 'Because ... because if you tell anyone ... and these children learn of the truth, then you know what will happen, don't you?' (p. 23) The use of ellipsis indicates that she is hesitating, as though making up the superstition as she speaks – or, perhaps, asking herself if it is wrong to employ such an extreme measure.

KEY CHARACTER: MR LYONS (A01)

Mr Lyons makes only a small number of appearances in the play. His frequent absence perhaps reflects the traditional middle class family structure in which Edward will grow up: the husband is at work all day, and absent for longer periods when work demands it, in order to provide money while the wife stays at home to look after the children. As Mr Lyons says to Mrs Lyons in this section: 'The house is your domain' (p. 21). He then hands over fifty pounds in cash which, unknown to him, will be used to pay off Mrs Johnstone.

His absence is also, of course, essential to the plot: Russell needs him to be 'away' at the start of the play in order to be unaware of Mrs Lyons's and Mrs Johnstone's agreement – and unaware that Mrs Lyons is not in fact pregnant.

KEY CONTEXT (A03)

The different roles of men and women, husbands and wives, were much more clearly defined in the 1950s when this section of the play is set – and to an extent in the 1980s when the play was written – than they are today.

EXAM FOCUS: WRITING ABOUT CHARACTER (A01)

You may be asked to write about the ways in which Russell presents characters in the play. Read this example of a student's response to Russell's presentation of Mrs Johnstone in this section:

> When Mrs Lyons sacks Mrs Johnstone and threatens her with superstition, Russell seems to be presenting Mrs Johnstone as totally helpless and vulnerable. She believes Mrs Lyons's made-up superstition and accepts her dismissal without question. She tries to take her baby back but immediately gives in when Mrs Lyons tells her she will be 'locked up' for giving her baby away. Russell has put Mrs Johnstone in circumstances which she seems powerless to change.

A clear statement about how Russell presents character

Evidence of how the author achieves this

Sums up the author's intention

Now you try it:

Complete this paragraph by adding one or two sentences about how the audience might respond to Russell's presentation of Mrs Johnstone.

ACT ONE, PART 5: THE TWINS ARE REUNITED (PP. 24–34)

SUMMARY

- Mickey, now aged seven, has been playing in the street, near the big houses. His mother reminds him that he is not allowed to play there, but will not explain why.
- Mickey sings about the problems of being seven and his respect for his older brother Sammy.
- Mickey and Edward meet by chance, and have no idea that they are related. Edward is impressed by Mickey and shares his sweets with him. When they discover they share a birthday, they agree to become blood brothers: a friendship cemented by sharing blood from a nick in their hands which Mickey makes with a penknife.
- Sammy appears and laughs at Edward and Mickey.
- Mrs Johnstone arrives and, realising who Mickey is playing with, sends Mickey into the house and sends Edward home, telling him never to come back.

WHY IS THIS SECTION IMPORTANT?

A Mickey and Edward are **reunited** for the first time since birth.
B Ironically, they decide to become **blood brothers**.
C Mrs Johnstone is shown trying to keep to her **agreement** with Mrs Lyons by keeping the boys **apart**.

KEY CHARACTERS: EDWARD AND MICKEY (A01)

Russell uses Mickey and Edward's differences to emphasise each one's individual character. The audience is first introduced to the seven-year-old Mickey in this section, singing about his respect for his older brother Sammy, because he can 'spit, / Straight in y' eye from twenty yards' and he urinates 'straight through the letter box / Of the house next door' (pp. 26–7). This is a strong indication of what is considered admirable in Mickey's world.

Edward, however, is much more naive and kind-hearted. He immediately agrees to Mickey's request to 'Gis a sweet' (p. 27), much to Mickey's amazement. He is delighted with Mickey's bad language and his story about the plate in his brother Sammy's head. Within minutes of being reunited, Mickey and Edward are best friends – but Russell then develops this dramatic irony by making the twins become blood brothers.

KEY THEME: CLASS (A02)

Mickey's conversation with his mother reveals that while they do not live 'down at the rough end' (p. 25), the Lyons live in one of the 'big houses' at 'the other end' (p. 25). Where they live represents the layers in society: the poorest at one end, the wealthy at the other.

KEY QUOTATION: THE 'F' WORD (A01)

A key moment that reveals Mickey's and Edward's similarities and differences is their discussion about 'the "F" word' (p. 28). Edward happily admits he has no idea what this is or what it means. Mickey knows the word, but not its meaning. Edward says he will look it up in the dictionary – which Mickey, though he is reluctant to admit it, does not know about: 'It's a, it's a thingy, innit?' (p. 29).

What each child knows and is familiar with – and what each one has not encountered yet – clearly illustrates the different worlds in which they live.

KEY LANGUAGE: DIALECT AND ACCENT (A02)

Each of the twins' language reflects their home environments. Like Mrs Johnstone's, Mickey's speech is full of abbreviations, contractions and language choices suggesting his Liverpool dialect and accent: 'y' have to be dead careful if our Sammy gives y' a sweet' (p. 28). Like Mrs Lyons's, Edward's speech is in standard English and is much more formal. He refers to 'my mummy' while Mickey talks about 'me mam' (p. 27). Sammy immediately recognises that Edward is a 'poshy' (p. 31) having heard him speak just one line.

However, Russell also uses language choice to show the similarities between the two boys and their friendship as Mickey draws Edward into his world: Edward is delighted by the rude words that Mickey knows and uses; Mickey starts calling him 'Eddie' (p. 30).

KEY CONTEXT (A03)

In the 1950s and 1960s, class divisions between the working class, middle class and upper class were much clearer than they are today. Each could be defined in terms of money, education, employment, housing, etc.

KEY FORM: ADULTS PLAYING CHILDREN (A02)

The roles of Mickey and Edward are usually played by the same two actors from the age of seven to their deaths. Their growing up is suggested through Russell's language choices and through costume. While much of the humour in this section comes from its content – for example, Mickey's ambitions to be like his brother, his discussion with Edward about the plate in his brother's head – the humour is significantly increased in performance by the fact that these lines and actions are being performed by two adult actors, sniggering at swear words, pretending to be seven, and wishing they were eight.

REVISION FOCUS: MICKEY AND EDWARD'S SIMILARITIES AND DIFFERENCES

Make a list of all the ways in which Mickey and Edward are different. You could think about the way they act, the way they talk, and the things they talk about. Make another list of the ways in which they are similar. Do you think they are more similar than different, or more different than similar?

ACT ONE, PART 6: MICKEY VISITS EDWARD'S HOUSE (PP. 34–7)

SUMMARY

- Edward returns home, where his father gives him a toy gun and reads him a story.
- Edward looks up 'bogey man' in the dictionary. His mother dismisses it as a 'superstition' that a 'silly mother' (p. 35) might use to frighten her children.
- Mickey calls round to see Edward but Mrs Lyons sends him away, saying it is Edward's bedtime.
- Mrs Lyons realises who Mickey is and scolds Edward for playing with him.
- Upset and angry, Edward swears inexpertly at his mother.
- Mrs Lyons hits Edward 'instinctively' (p. 37) and immediately regrets it. She sees Edward's swearing as a direct result of Mickey's bad influence.

CHECKPOINT 6 **A01**

Mr Lyons gives Edward a gun at the start of this section and Edward is 'delighted' (p. 34). In what way does this link Edward to other characters in the play?

WHY IS THIS SECTION IMPORTANT?

A The character of Mrs Lyons is presented in an ambiguous light: her actions are clearly **reprehensible** but the audience may have some **sympathy** with her motives.

B Russell develops the **parallels** between Mickey and Edward while emphasising their **differences**.

KEY CHARACTER: MRS LYONS A01

Mrs Lyons hits her son, Edward, in this section. The stage directions say she hits him *'instinctively'* (p. 37), suggesting that this is the result of frustration or anger beyond her control. Could this be the first signs of the mental illness that is suggested later in the play when she threatens Mrs Johnstone with a knife? Or the result of her desperate desire to make Edward her own 'beautiful son' (p. 37) and not Mrs Johnstone's? Or her anger at Mickey for tainting her son with his 'filth' (p. 37)? All of these possible interpretations contribute to Russell's development of Mrs Lyons as a complex character in a complex situation.

KEY THEME: PARENTS AND CHILDREN A01

Mrs Lyons's main concern throughout the play is to ensure that the only influence on Edward is hers and her husband's – and to prevent Mickey and his family having any influence on him at all.

Mrs Lyons could be seen as a domineering and controlling parent. This is in strong contrast to Mrs Johnstone, who struggles to control her children's behaviour, to feed them and to manage the debt she creates by buying them what they demand. Mrs Lyons's overpowering desire to protect her son from harm makes it all the more shocking (and ironic) that she hits him.

KEY QUOTATION: 'I LIKE HIM MORE THAN YOU' A01

Edward is so angered by his mother's refusal to let him play with Mickey that he tries to punish her, saying, 'I like him more than you' (p. 36). While this may be a frustrated outburst typical of a seven year old, it immediately suggests (at least to Mrs Lyons) that Edward feels a stronger bond with his natural brother than with his adoptive mother. When he swears at her using language he has learned from that brother, it seems to confirm her fears: her influence over Edward is not as strong as the influence of his birth family.

CHECKPOINT 7 A02

Note down two different ways in which an audience might react to Edward's swearing.

AIMING HIGH: NATURE OR NURTURE?

The play encourages the audience to ask themselves questions about **nature** (those parts of our personalities with which we are born) and **nurture** (the influence that our parents and our home lives have on us).

There is clear evidence that Mickey's language and behaviour have a strong influence on Edward when he swears at his mother. However, there is no evidence that Edward has any significant influence on Mickey. Could Russell be suggesting that, despite Mrs Lyons's efforts to nurture Edward as a 'nice polite middle-class boy', he easily reverts to his true nature as a member of the Johnstone family?

TOP TIP (A01)

Although Linda could be considered a secondary character in the play, her significance in the lives and deaths of Mickey and Edward should not be underestimated.

ACT ONE, PART 7: CAUGHT BY THE POLICE (PP. 37–48)

SUMMARY

- Mickey, Linda, Sammy and other children play in the street while Edward watches from the safety of his back garden. The game dissolves into disagreement between Mickey and Linda's gang and Sammy's gang.
- Mickey has discovered where Sammy hides his airgun, and shows the gun to Linda.
- Mickey calls to Edward to come and play. Both say their mothers have forbidden them to play with each other but decide to 'take no notice' (p. 42).
- Mickey and Linda suggest going to the park to fire the airgun. Edward is worried that a policeman might catch them, but is impressed when Mickey and Linda explain how disrespectful they are to policemen.
- Mrs Lyons is worried when she cannot find Edward. Mr Lyons tries to reassure her, but she says she wants to move away and is worried about the people that Edward is mixing with.
- Mr Lyons is concerned by Mrs Lyons's over-reaction and thinks she should see a doctor.
- Mickey, Linda and Edward are firing the airgun and throwing stones in the park when a policeman arrives. Edward is impertinent to the policeman, but starts to cry when he begins to realise he is in trouble. Mickey and Linda are soon crying too.
- The policeman visits Mrs Johnstone. He reminds her of previous warnings he has given her about her children's behaviour and says that next time it will end in a court appearance. Mrs Johnstone wishes she could move house and start a new life.
- The policeman visits Mrs Lyons and suggests she dock Edward's pocket money and stop him mixing with children like Mickey and Linda.

WHY IS THIS SECTION IMPORTANT?

A The play's **ending** is foreshadowed in Mickey and Sammy's **shooting games** and Mickey taking Sammy's **airgun** from its hiding place.

B It emphasises that Mickey and Edward are **inseparable**, despite the best efforts of Mrs Johnstone and Mrs Lyons.

C Mr Lyons suggests that Mrs Lyons's **mental health** is deteriorating.

D It shows how easily Mickey can **influence** Edward's behaviour – and how **naive** Edward is.

KEY THEME: CLASS (A02)

In this section, Russell uses stereotypes of class to create humour. Mickey lives up to the stereotype of the lower class, bragging about his disrespect for the police – but his bragging and the stereotype are soon overturned and Mickey ends the scene in tears. Edward is perhaps more typical of the middle class stereotype – a naive boy who believes Mickey's every word with no idea of the consequences of being impertinent to a policeman.

TOP TIP (A01)

Beware of commenting on the stereotypical characteristics of 'the rich' and 'the poor', or the 'lower class' and 'middle class'. Think about how Russell uses stereotypes – but avoid stereotypical responses to the characters in *Blood Brothers*.

KEY THEME: SUPERSTITION (A02)

Earlier in Act One, Mrs Lyons laughed at Mrs Johnstone's superstition about putting new shoes on a table. However, in this section of the play, Mrs Lyons seems to have become superstitious herself. She is alarmed when Mr Lyons puts a pair of Edward's shoes on the table: '*She rushes at the table and sweeps the shoes off*' (p. 45). Her fear that 'something terrible will happen' (p. 45) if they do not move away suggests that she has even come to believe her own invented superstition that the twins will die if they are told the truth. Mr Lyons's suggestion that she 'should see a doctor' (p. 45) implies that this change is the result of her deteriorating mental health. Ironically, the audience already knows that she is right: the twins will die.

KEY THEME: FATE (A02)

When the Narrator reveals the play's ending in its first few lines, Russell creates the impression that the twins' fate is sealed: it is their destiny to die. He reinforces this impression throughout the play. In this section, for example, Mrs Lyons is convinced that, if they do not move away and remove Edward from the influence of the Johnstones, then 'something terrible will happen, something bad' (p. 45). Immediately after this scene, as at several other key moments in the play, the Narrator echoes her ominous prediction with his song, 'There's shoes upon the table ...' (p. 45).

> **KEY CONTEXT** (A03)
>
> Shakespeare uses a similar technique to Russell in *Macbeth*: the witches' prediction of Macbeth's fate haunts him throughout the play and proves to be accurate.

EXAM FOCUS: WRITING ABOUT THE PLAY'S STRUCTURE (A01)

You might be asked to write about the play's structure. Read this student's comments on structure in response to a question about the theme of fate.

Expresses a clear point	As well as helping the audience to follow the story, the Narrator is an important part of the structure of 'Blood Brothers'. At key points in the play, he sings the same song, 'There's shoes upon the table ...' to remind the audience that the play will end tragically and the twins will die. Russell does this to build tension and make it feel like everything in the play is building up to the moment of Mickey and Edward's death.

Expresses a clear point

Comments on its effect

Supported with evidence from the text

Comments on the impact of the writer's choices

Now you try it:

Add to this answer by saying something about how Russell uses song at the end of the play.

ACT ONE, PART 8: MOVING AWAY (PP. 48–58)

SUMMARY

- Mr and Mrs Lyons are moving house, from the town to the country.
- Edward goes to say goodbye to Mrs Johnstone. She comforts him because he is upset, saying he wants to stay near Mickey and will never forget him.
- Mrs Johnstone gives Edward a locket containing a picture of her and Mickey, and tells him to keep it a secret.
- Edward gives Mickey a present: a toy gun.
- The Lyons move into their new house in the country. Edward is worried when he sees a magpie.
- Mickey and Edward sing, revealing their loneliness and that each is missing the other.
- The Johnstones are also moving to 'Where nobody's heard of our name' and are 'startin' all over again' (p. 57).

WHY IS THIS SECTION IMPORTANT?

A Edward and Mickey's lives continue to **mirror** each other as both families **move** to the country.

B Mickey's **influence** over Edward is still apparent, despite the move.

C The **locket** that Mrs Johnstone gives to Edward symbolises their **relationship** and will have an important function in Act Two.

KEY SETTING: THE COUNTRY   (A02)

Both families move away from Liverpool at the end of Act One. Both hope to start a new life: the Lyons think they are escaping the Johnstones and cutting Edward's ties with them; Mrs Johnstone thinks her family are escaping their reputation and can make a new start.

The audience was shown at the start of Act One, and is reminded throughout, that the twins cannot escape their destiny. In the light of this, both families moving to the country and dreaming of escape is highly ironic, undercutting the positive moods of Mrs Johnstone and Mrs Lyons.

AIMING HIGH: WHY MOVE THE FAMILIES?

Make sure you can discuss the reasons behind Russell's choices as a writer. Many of his decisions are taken for reasons of character or plot development. For example, Russell uses the locket in Act Two to allow Mrs Lyons to discover that Edward has been in touch with Mrs Johnstone, and to drive Mrs Lyons to further despair. However, moving both families to the country is not simply a question of plot development. Russell could have kept both families in Liverpool without any impact on the plot or his characters. It seems that this decision was made purely to highlight how neither can escape the other or their fate.

CHECKPOINT 8 (A02)

In performance, the set is not usually changed in Act Two: the inside of Mrs Lyons's house and the outside of Mrs Johnstone's house look the same even though they have moved. What does this suggest about their new lives?

KEY LANGUAGE: THE USE OF SYMBOLS (A02)

The locket, which contains a picture of Mrs Johnstone and Mickey, and which Mrs Johnstone removes from her own neck and gives to Edward is a symbol of her true relationship to Edward and his belonging to her and her family. However, Russell gives it more significance in Act Two: it plays a role in Edward's suspension from school (in parallel to Mickey's suspension from his school) and is the means by which Mrs Lyons discovers that Edward has been in contact with Mrs Johnstone.

TOP TIP: WRITING ABOUT SUPERSTITION (A02)

Look at how Russell uses superstition in this section. Edward is upset when he sees a single magpie, explaining that it means that sorrow will follow – which the audience knows it eventually will. His father tells him it's just a 'stupid superstition' (p. 52), echoing his mother's comments about the 'bogey man' (p. 35) in Act One, Part 6. As with the superstition of the bogey man, Edward says it's not stupid because Mickey told him about it. This happens apparently within minutes of the Lyons arriving at their new home, ironically highlighting to Mrs Lyons – and the audience – that it will take more than a move to the country to remove Mickey's influence over Edward.

AIMING HIGH: THE ROLE OF MOTIFS

Note that guns appear several times during Act One, for example in Mickey and Sammy's games and when Mickey and Edward play with Sammy's airgun and are caught by the policeman. In this section, Edward gives Mickey a toy gun as a leaving present. In Act One, Part 6, Edward's father gave him a present of a toy gun. Perhaps Russell is suggesting that this is the same gun, given once as a token of family love and now again for similar reasons, although Mickey and Edward do not know it.

The recurring motif of guns is, of course, a significant reminder that real guns will play a part in the twins' deaths, as re-enacted at the start of the play. Is Russell, perhaps, pointing out the consequences of children playing with, and not recognising the dangers of, guns? Or is he using them to build tension as the play progresses to its inevitable resolution?

REVISION FOCUS: SUPERSTITION

Note down all the references to, and examples of, superstition throughout Act One. What do they suggest about Edward and Mickey, and Mrs Johnstone and Mrs Lyons, and how they influence each other's lives?

TOP TIP (A02)

It could be argued that Willy Russell is suggesting in *Blood Brothers* that we should take superstitions seriously. However, it is much more important to consider **how** and **why** he uses superstition to manipulate the plot of the play and the audience's response to it.

CHECKPOINT 9

Who does Mrs Johnstone blame for Sammy's school being burned down?

ACT TWO, PART 1: A NEW START (PP. 59–62)

SUMMARY

- In her new home, Mrs Johnstone sings a song about her noisy neighbours and the fact that she is up to date with her bills and has been out dancing with Joe, the Milkman.
- Sammy has burnt his school down and been put on probation.
- Mrs Johnstone describes Mickey's interest in girls.
- Edward, meanwhile, is practising the waltz with his mother and complains that he hardly ever sees girls when he is at his single-sex boarding school.
- Edward returns to school.
- Mrs Johnstone tells Mickey he is going to miss the school bus and teases him that he has been talking about Linda in his sleep.

WHY IS THIS SECTION IMPORTANT?

A   It shows that some **elements** of Mrs Johnstone's life have changed for the **better** – but some have not.

B   Mickey and Edward's **teenage lives** are directly **contrasted**.

C   Mickey's **teenage relationship** with **Linda** is introduced.

KEY CONTEXT

The Johnstone's new home is in Skelmersdale, Lancashire, which was designated a 'new town' in 1961. A large amount of housing was built and many people moved there from Liverpool.

KEY CHARACTERS: MICKEY AND EDWARD

As at several other points in the play, Russell highlights parallels in, and encourages direct comparisons of, Mickey and Edward's lives. Both are preparing for school: Mickey is being hurried by his mother to get the bus to the local school; Edward is being driven by his father to his boys' boarding school and will not return until half term. Both are showing an interest in girls: Mickey denies that he is interested in Linda; Edward complains that he hardly ever sees a girl when he is at school.

KEY FORM: HUMOUR **A02**

Despite the tragic form of *Blood Brothers* (see **Themes: Fate and superstition**), Russell makes frequent use of humour. At the start of Act Two, Mrs Johnstone's song contrasts her happiness in her new life with some very familiar elements of her old life in Liverpool, to great comic effect.

She says the neighbours are 'a treat' (p. 59) because they only fight at the weekends – and is interrupted by loud shouting from next door. She can now pay the Milkman and has even been dancing with him – unlike the Milkman in Act One who was the first to complain to her that he had not been paid. However, this happiness is soon contrasted with the news that Sammy has 'burnt the school down' (p. 59). Perhaps Russell is using the humour in these contrasts to make a serious point: you can change where you live, but you cannot change your family or your class.

> **TOP TIP**
>
> What would be lost if Sammy did not appear in the play? How could Russell have achieved these plot and character developments without him?

AIMING HIGH: THE MOTIF OF DANCING

Notice how Russell uses motifs throughout the play. The act of dancing, for example, is used to suggest happiness. At the beginning of Act One, Mrs Johnstone recalls dancing with her husband when they first met and at their wedding. Significantly the dancing stopped when her children were born. At the beginning of Act Two, Mrs Johnstone says she has been dancing with Joe the Milkman, suggesting she has started a new and successful relationship as part of her new life.

A few lines later, we see Mrs Lyons trying to dance with 'a very awkward' (p. 61) Edward as she teaches him the waltz. This seems to reflect her relationship with Edward: she guides and teaches him in a formal and controlled dance in the same way that she guides him through his very formal and controlled childhood.

ACT TWO, PART 2: SUSPENSIONS AND SECRETS (PP. 63–70)

SUMMARY

- Mrs Johnstone waves Mickey and Sammy off on the bus. The conductor sings a song, warning her that the past cannot be 'Wiped out' and 'forgotten' (p. 63).
- Sammy tries to buy a child's ticket on the bus and argues with the bus conductor. Sammy pulls a knife and threatens the conductor. He jumps from the bus and runs, chased by the police.
- Linda tells Mickey she loves him and Mickey complains that she says it all the time. They leave for school.
- Meanwhile a teacher at Edward's private boarding school tries to confiscate the locket he is wearing. Edward swears at him, refuses to hand it over and is suspended as a result.
- Mickey and Linda are in a lesson at their secondary modern school. Mickey does not know the answer to one of the teacher's questions and therefore argues with, and mocks, him. He is sent out of the lesson. When Linda stands up for him, she too is sent out. Both are suspended.
- Mrs Lyons reads a letter about Edward's suspension and asks about the locket. Edward shows it to her but will not tell her where he got it.
- Mrs Lyons opens the locket and thinks it contains a picture of Edward and Mrs Johnstone.
- Edward explains that the picture is of Mickey and Mrs Johnstone but will not confess how he got the locket.
- The Narrator sings a song reminding us that the past cannot be 'brushed away' (p. 69).

WHY IS THIS SECTION IMPORTANT?

A It reminds the audience that the **events** of the **past** will have **significant consequences** in the characters' **futures**.

B It reiterates the **bond** between Edward and Mickey and Mrs Johnstone and the **impact** this has on Mrs Lyons.

C It emphasises the **similarities** in Mickey and Edward's lives.

KEY CHARACTERS: MICKEY AND EDWARD (A01)

Once again, Russell creates clear parallels – and invites direct comparisons – between Mickey and Edward in this section. Despite their different schools, both boys challenge their teachers and are suspended. Now aged fourteen, both are much more confident and skilled in tackling authority. The last time that they attempted it – when they were caught throwing stones by a policeman – both of the twins ended up in tears. As before, though, it is Edward's connection with Mickey and Mrs Johnstone that leads him into trouble.

KEY THEME: FATE (A02)

Twice in this section – after Mrs Johnstone happily waves her sons off on the school bus and again after Edward will not tell Mrs Lyons where he got the locket – the Narrator reminds them and the audience that the past cannot be 'forgotten' (p. 63) or 'brushed away' (p. 69).

However, in this section he does not just sing about 'shoes upon the table' or 'walkin' on pavement cracks' (Act One, p. 45). Here he suggests that it is not superstitious fate but the choices these characters made in the past that will lead to the play's resolution – and that 'the price' of those choices must be 'paid' (p. 63).

KEY QUOTATION: SECRETS (A01)

In the final scene of this section, Edward refuses to tell his mother where he got the locket he wears: 'it's a secret' (p. 69). This scene is heavy with dramatic irony. Mrs Lyons tries to persuade Edward, reminding him, 'I'm your mother' (p. 69) – which of course she isn't. Edward argues that he should be allowed to keep his secret: he says to Mrs Lyons, 'everybody has secrets, don't you have secrets?' (p. 70). Russell uses the repetition of 'secrets' to emphasise that, Mrs Lyons herself is concealing the truth: the woman whose picture is inside the locket is Edward's biological mother, Mrs Johnstone.

TOP TIP (A01)

When writing about Edward and Mrs Johnstone, avoid referring to her as 'Edward's real mother' – use the term 'biological mother' instead.

EXAM FOCUS: WRITING ABOUT THEMES (A01)

You may be asked to write about the ways in which Russell presents a key theme in the play. Read this example of a student's response to Russell's presentation of the theme of secrets in this section:

A clear statement about the impact of this theme on the play as a whole

The plot of the entire play depends on people keeping secrets. For example, if Mrs Johnstone and Mrs Lyons told Mickey and Edward that they were twins it would change their relationship and their lives and almost certainly the ending of the play. When Edward will not tell Mrs Lyons where he got his locket, it makes her even more jealous and desperate to protect Edward from Mickey and Mrs Johnstone.

Supported with examples

A specific example and the impact it has on one character

Now you try it:

Complete this paragraph by adding one or two sentences about how Russell presents the scene where Mrs Lyons questions Edward about his locket. You could, for example, write about how the secrets that the characters keep lead directly to the play's ending.

ACT TWO, PART 3: MICKEY AND EDWARD REUNITED (PP. 70–7)

SUMMARY

- Mickey and Linda are walking in the countryside. Mickey is too shy to tell her how he feels about her.
- As Edward approaches, both twins sing a song that reveals their lack of self-confidence and jealousy of the other's confidence and good looks.
- The twins recognise each other.
- Mickey explains that he cannot tell Linda about his feelings for her. The boys decide it may help if they go to see *Nymphomaniac Nights* and *Swedish Au Pairs* at the cinema.
- The boys go to Mickey's house so he can get some money for the cinema from his mother – but Mrs Lyons has spotted them together and follows them.
- Mrs Johnstone finds out which films the boys are going to see and laughs at them.

WHY IS THIS SECTION IMPORTANT?

A Mickey and Edward's characters have **developed** as they become **teenagers**.

B Mickey's **relationship** with Linda is **explored**.

C It raises questions about Mrs Johnstone's **parenting of her children**.

KEY CONTEXT (A03)

The relaxation of obscenity and censorship laws in the 1960s resulted in pornographic films being shown in cinemas in the 1960s and 1970s. The fictional titles of the two pornographic films that Mickey and Edward watch are typical of the time.

KEY THEME: GROWING UP (A02)

Mickey and Edward are growing up. Although their home lives are very different, Russell continues to highlight parallels in their characters. Both lack self-confidence, singing of their doubts about themselves and how, when they see but have not yet recognised each other, they wish they could be more 'like / That guy' (p. 72). Ironically, of course, they are twins and look alike.

These issues of confidence are particularly apparent in Mickey's relationship with Linda. She does her best to get him to put his arms around her, and make him jealous, saying that a boy they see (who turns out to be Edward) is 'gorgeous' (p. 71). However, it is only when she walks off in frustration that Mickey can express his feelings: 'Linda, I wanna kiss y' … but I don't know how to tell y' ' (p. 71).

Although he has no girlfriend and goes to a single-sex boarding school, Edward appears confident in giving Mickey advice about girls because he has 'read about it' (p. 74). He advises Mickey to tell Linda that, 'the very core of my being is longing for you' (p. 74), his language choice suggesting, for comic effect, that his knowledge of romance is entirely based on things he has read in 'magazines' (p. 71). Perhaps, in reality, Edward would be just as awkward if he met a girl.

KEY THEME: PARENTS AND CHILDREN (A02)

Mrs Johnstone sees through Mickey and Edward's lies about the films they are going to see at the cinema. Her reaction, though, is revealing. She laughs at the boys and very quickly 'gets on with her work' (p. 77). Edward thinks that she is 'fabulous' (p. 77) having such a relaxed attitude – perhaps in contrast to the reaction he might expect from Mrs Lyons. It could, however, be argued that her attitude is irresponsible and inappropriate.

Mickey and Edward's descriptions of their mothers are similar in this section. Mickey says his mum is a 'headcase' (p. 77). Edward describes his mother as 'off her beam' (p. 75). While both descriptions suggest mental illness, in Mickey's case this seems to be a compliment, implying that Mrs Johnstone is funny and eccentric. In contrast, Edward may be suggesting that Mrs Lyons's deteriorating mental health is resulting in unpredictable and irrational thoughts and actions – as supported by events in the next scene.

REVISION FOCUS: MRS JOHNSTONE'S DECISIONS

Write down all the decisions Mrs Johnstone has made as a parent in the play so far. Which of her decisions is she forced to make through circumstance and which does she choose to make? Do you think Russell intends her to be seen as a good parent? Note down your answers to these questions.

> **TOP TIP** (A01)
>
> Be careful not to make moral judgements about characters when you write about the play. Rather than suggesting it is a fact that *Mrs Johnstone is a bad parent*, express it as a possible response to Russell's presentation of character: *It could be argued that Mrs Johnstone is presented as a bad parent.*

CHECKPOINT 10

Why does Mrs Johnstone say she does not want to take any more money from Mrs Lyons?

ACT TWO, PART 4: TEENAGE YEARS (PP. 77–87)

SUMMARY

- Mrs Lyons confronts Mrs Johnstone in her kitchen, accusing her of moving house in order to follow her. She offers Mrs Johnstone money to move away, but it is turned down.

- Mrs Lyons tries to attack Mrs Johnstone with a kitchen knife, but Mrs Johnstone manages to disarm her.

- Mickey and Edward come out of the cinema and meet Linda and her friend who have been to see the same film. Mickey, Edward and Linda are disrespectful to a policeman and then run off.

- In a condensed sequence of events, we see Mickey, Edward and Linda spend their teenage years together: at the fairground, in the chip shop and on the beach.

- Linda and Edward talk while Mickey is at work. Edward tells her that he is leaving for university the next day and asks if he can write to her. She agrees.

- Mickey has still not told Linda of his feelings for her. Edward's song suggests that he too has feelings for her, which he would make clear if it were not for Mickey.

- With Edward's encouragement, Mickey kisses Linda.

WHY IS THIS SECTION IMPORTANT?

A   The **breakdown** of Mrs Lyons's **mental health** is becoming more apparent.
B   **Time** moves on. Mickey, Edward and Linda are now **young adults**.
C   Mickey finally **reveals** his **feelings** to Linda.

KEY QUOTATION: 'I NEVER MADE HIM MINE' A01

The scene in which Mrs Lyons confronts Mrs Johnstone is highly dramatic. Almost immediately Mrs Lyons accuses Mrs Johnstone of moving house because of Edward: 'Are you always going to follow me?' (p. 77). Note that Russell gives her the word 'me' not 'Edward', suggesting that she thinks Mrs Johnstone is following her in order to persecute her rather than following Edward to be near him. This suggestion of paranoia becomes more apparent when she describes how: 'when he was a tiny baby I'd see him looking straight at me and I'd think, he knows … he knows' (p. 78). He could not, of course, have possibly known as a baby and still does not at this point in the play.

Mrs Lyons seems haunted by the idea that Edward is closer to his birth family than to her, 'I took him. But I never made him mine' (p. 78). This implies that, despite her best efforts to be Edward's mother, Mrs Lyons feels he is still Mrs Johnstone's son and not her own.

KEY CHARACTER: MRS LYONS

At this point in the play, audiences may respond to the character of Mrs Lyons in a number of different ways. Her sadness that she does not feel her son truly belongs to her might prompt sympathy, or even pity. However, her attack on Mrs Johnstone again casts her in the light of villain, despite the circumstances and feelings that have driven her to such desperation.

It is made clear that, when the Lyons first moved, Edward 'talked less and less of you and your family' (p. 78) suggesting that, if the twins had not met again, they may have forgotten each other. Perhaps ultimately, then, Mrs Lyons is a victim of her circumstances, tormented by the constant coinciding of her family's and the Johnstone family's lives.

KEY STRUCTURE: THE YEARS GO BY

Earlier in the play, the years between the twins' birth and the age of seven are skipped over. Similarly, the years between seven and fourteen are omitted in the interval between Act One and Act Two. In this section, however, the years between the ages of fourteen and eighteen (suggested by Edward leaving for university) are not skipped over but condensed.

In the montage sequence of scenes from their teenage years, Russell emphasises the closeness of Mickey, Edward and Linda's friendship. We see them as a trio of friends, rather than as a couple – Mickey and Linda – and their friend, Edward. This is, perhaps, why Russell decided that Mickey should be too shy to tell Linda his feelings for such a long time. If Mickey and Linda had become boyfriend and girlfriend much earlier in the play, it would have weakened the relationship between Mickey and Edward – both as friends and as parallel characters in the play, moving relentlessly towards their shared fate.

> **CHECKPOINT 11** (A01)
>
> Which **two** pieces of information reveal to the audience that Mickey and Edward have now left school and become adults?

TOP TIP: WRITING ABOUT EDWARD (A01)

Notice how Edward seems much more confident than Mickey in this section. He dances with Linda's friend, he is the first to be impertinent to the policeman, he sings that he would have no hesitation in expressing his feelings for Linda if he were Mickey. In the text there is no obvious evidence for his growing confidence. Perhaps it is implied that his middle class upbringing or private education has made him more confident. Perhaps it is also in the interests of the plot and the plausibility of the play: Russell needs Edward to display the qualities which will allow him to become an influential politician when he leaves university – placing him in even starker contrast to Mickey.

ACT TWO, PART 5: ADULT LIFE (PP. 87–95)

SUMMARY

- Mickey tells his mother that Linda is pregnant and that he and Linda plan to get married before Christmas.
- Mickey says that they are making people redundant at the factory where he works.
- As Mr Lyons sings about these redundancies, Mickey and Linda are married.
- Edward returns from university and finds that Mickey is troubled by the adult responsibilities of work and redundancy. Mickey says that Edward has not grown up yet.
- Edward confesses to Linda that he loves her. She tells him that she is pregnant and that she and Mickey are married.
- Mickey agrees to be a lookout for Sammy at a robbery he has planned.

CHECKPOINT 12 (A02)

At the start of this section, the Narrator describes the month and the season ('It was one day in October …/ And winter broke the promise that the summer had just made' (p. 87)). Why is this significant?

WHY IS THIS SECTION IMPORTANT?

A It shows a **significant change** in Mickey and Linda's lives.
B It shows a **significant change** in Mickey and Edward's relationship.
C It establishes the **situation** which will, ultimately, lead directly to the twins' **deaths**.

TOP TIP: WRITING ABOUT JUXTAPOSITION (A02)

Notice how, throughout this section, Russell uses juxtaposition to highlight Mickey's situation.

Russell places Mr Lyons's song, 'Take a letter Miss Jones' (p. 89), in direct juxtaposition with Mickey and Linda's wedding, contrasting the misery of unemployment with the expected joy of a wedding, a pregnancy, and Christmas approaching. In performance, the song's music – fast and upbeat – also contrasts sharply with the content of its lyrics, suggesting that Mr Lyons is, at best, dismissing the redundancies as just 'a sign / Of the times' (p. 89) and, at worst, taking pleasure in them.

Russell further highlights his intended contrast with his stage directions: 'The Guests at the wedding become a line of men looking for work' (p. 89), queuing at the dole office to collect their unemployment benefit.

As Mickey finds himself unemployed with a wife and a child on the way, Russell further highlights his position by juxtaposing it with Edward's, just returned from a 'fantastic' (p. 91) time at university with a new group of 'tremendous' (p. 91) friends, looking forward to Christmas parties.

KEY THEME: POVERTY AND CRIME (A02)

The script implies that Mr Lyons is the managing director of the company that makes Mickey redundant. In one way, it is his redundancy that directly leads to Mickey's downfall – if he had a job, he would not be tempted to take part in the robbery Sammy has planned. Russell seems to suggest here that crime is a direct result of unemployment and poverty.

KEY THEME: GROWING UP (A02)

Mickey and Edward appear to have grown apart in this section. Whereas once Edward's naivety was used to create humour – for example, when Mickey helped himself to Edward's sweets – it now creates a divide between the twins. Mickey feels he has become an adult, while Edward is 'still a kid' (p. 92). Mickey points out that Edward cannot understand his situation, 'You don't understand anythin' do ye?' (p. 92), and dismisses their old relationship as 'kids' stuff' (p. 93).

How much things have changed is highlighted as Edward declares his love for Linda, learns that she has married Mickey and leaves her to be with his new friends. At the same time, Mickey is drawn into Sammy's crime as Linda calls after him, 'Mickey ... Mickey ... No!' (p. 95). The relationships of the past are changing and breaking down.

KEY CONTEXT (A03)

Unemployment was an extremely significant issue in Britain in the 1980s. In 1982 – the year of the first performance of *Blood Brothers* – unemployment reached a national total of three million, meaning that more than 10 per cent of people were out of work. In some parts of Liverpool, it was as high as 40 per cent.

ACT TWO, PART 6: CRIME AND PUNISHMENT (PP. 95–103)

SUMMARY

- The robbery at the filling station (petrol station) does not go according to plan and Sammy shoots someone.
- Mickey and Sammy run home. Linda arrives and Sammy hides his gun under a floorboard.
- When two policemen come to Mickey's house, Sammy runs out of the back door and is caught. Both he and Mickey are sent to prison.
- Mickey is prescribed pills for depression while in prison. Linda visits him and tries in vain to persuade him to stop taking them.
- Linda tells Mrs Johnstone that she has arranged a new house and a new job for Mickey, and that she hopes this will help Mickey stop taking the pills.
- Linda hides Mickey's pills but he insists that he has tried and failed to give them up. He guesses that his new job and house were arranged by Edward, who is now a local councillor.
- Linda meets Edward and they begin an affair.
- Mrs Lyons points out their affair to Mickey. Mickey takes the gun that Sammy hid under the floor, and goes after them. Mrs Johnstone calls him back but Mickey ignores her.

WHY IS THIS SECTION IMPORTANT?

A It highlights Mickey's **inability** to recover from his time in **prison**.

B Mickey's **failings** and Edward's **successes** are **contrasted** – and their **effect** on Mickey is emphasised.

C The play is reaching its **climax**.

KEY CHARACTER: MICKEY (A01)

The consequences of Mickey's crime and his imprisonment continue to resound and grow in this section. Russell uses Mickey's addiction to medication to highlight his feelings of inadequacy – particularly in light of Edward's role in getting him his new job and new house. Mickey compares their relationship now to their relationship in the past, pointing out that, 'It used to be just sweets an' ciggies he gave me ... Now it's a job and a house.' (p. 100), suggesting that Mickey's feelings of inadequacy are only increased by Edward's help – and his awareness that Edward's wealth and privilege have always given him opportunities that are unavailable to Mickey. Russell is, though, keen to highlight how 'determined' Mickey is to stop taking the pills, emphasising the 'strain' (p. 102) this causes him. One effect of this is to maintain the audience's sympathy for him – particularly as this is positioned immediately after the scene in which we see Edward and Linda's affair beginning.

KEY CONTEXT (A03)

There was a great deal of concern about the addictive nature of some antidepressants that were prescribed in the 1970s and 1980s.

KEY QUOTATION: INVISIBLE (A01)

Linda tells Mickey that when he takes his tablets, 'I can't even see you' (p. 100). Mickey's reply indicates that this is precisely why he takes them: to be 'invisible'. This exchange implies that the tablets change Mickey and prevent him from facing his failings and the frustration he feels with the world. This plays a significant part in the rage that overtakes him when he sees Linda with Edward.

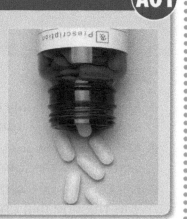

KEY CONTEXT (A03)

The actress and film star Marilyn Monroe died of a drugs overdose in 1963. Russell implies that Mickey's addiction will have similarly tragic consequences.

KEY CHARACTER: MRS LYONS (A01)

Russell gives Mrs Lyons the role of pointing out to Mickey that Edward and Linda are having an affair. This could have been achieved if Mickey had simply seen them by chance.

Following her attempt to stab Mrs Johnstone with a kitchen knife, this incident seems similarly to be borne out of bitterness – and is, ironically, the catalyst for events which will result in Edward's death. The fact that Mrs Lyons physically 'turns Mickey round' (p. 103) to see Edward and Linda together, without dialogue, suggests her manipulation of Mickey – and could make her actions seem still more sinister.

EXAM FOCUS: WRITING ABOUT CHARACTER (A02)

You may be asked to write about the ways in which Russell presents characters in the play. Read this example of a student's response to Russell's presentation of Mickey in this section:

> At the end of the play, Russell presents Mickey as a helpless and vulnerable character who wants to be 'invisible'. This adjective suggests that Mickey feels worthless and just wants to disappear. Mickey is shown desperately trying to get himself off the tablets but it is too late – Linda has already begun an affair with Edward. All of this builds the audience's sympathy for Mickey as his life disintegrates.

Supported with a quotation

Explores the writer's language choice

A clear statement about how Russell presents a character

Explains the author's intention

Now you try it:

Complete this paragraph by adding one or two sentences. You could write about how references to Marilyn Monroe contribute to the audience's thoughts and feelings about Mickey's situation.

ACT TWO, PART 7: THE END (PP. 103–8)

SUMMARY

- Mickey desperately roams the town, not sure what he is looking for or why, while Mrs Johnstone tries to catch up with him.
- Mrs Johnstone goes to tell Linda what Mickey is doing, and hurries with her to the Town Hall where Edward is giving a speech.
- Mickey appears with the gun trained on Edward. He says that Linda was the one thing he had left – and now Edward has taken her. Edward claims that he and Linda are just friends.
- Mickey suggests that Edward is the father of Linda's baby.
- Armed police marksmen arrive.
- Mrs Johnstone walks towards the platform and tells Mickey and Edward the truth: they are twins.
- Mickey is furious that she gave Edward away and not him. He fires the gun by mistake, killing Edward. The police marksmen shoot Mickey dead.
- The Narrator summarises the story of the play as he did at the beginning of Act One. Mrs Johnstone's final song expresses her shock and disbelief at the death of the twins.

TOP TIP (A01)

Think carefully about Mickey's reasons for pointing a gun at Edward. There is not one simple explanation but a complex web of circumstances which lead to the twins' tragic deaths.

WHY IS THIS SECTION IMPORTANT?

A   Mickey explains why he is so **hurt** by Edward's **affair** with Linda.
B   The story's **ending** – highlighted at the beginning, and throughout the drama – is finally **played out**.

KEY THEME: SUPERSTITION AND CLASS (A02)

In his final speech, the Narrator seems to contradict – or at least throw doubt on – what has led to the events of this final section of the play. 'And do we blame superstition for what came to pass? / Or could it be what we, the English, have come to know as class?' (p. 107)

Although Russell has used the Narrator and the concept of superstition to build tension and create the suggestion of fate controlling the lives of his characters, here he seems to suggest that it is the differences in the twins' upbringings that has brought them to this ending. The play does present a clearly widening gap between the twins as their lives take very different directions: Edward's to university and a position of wealth and power; Mickey's to poverty, crime and a dependency on prescription drugs; and Russell suggests that it is these paths that lead directly to the twins' deaths.

KEY QUOTATION: EVERYTHING AND NOTHING (A01)

Mickey's fury at Edward is summed up in one line: 'how come you got everything ... an' I got nothin'?' (p. 105), the contrast between 'everything' and 'nothin'' emphasising Mickey's fury at the differences in their lives. His bitterness resurfaces shortly before he shoots Edward, as he rages at his mother for keeping him: 'Why didn't you give me away? ... I could have been ... I could have been him!' (p. 106), suggesting that the only thing that has made their lives so different is their upbringing.

However, Russell focuses Mickey's anger on the loss of Linda, and the thought that his baby may be Edward's. It could be that this is the final straw that drives him to these desperate measures: not the differences in their upbringing, or their opportunities in life, but the loss of his love: the 'one thing I had left' (p. 105).

REVISION FOCUS: TRACKING EVENTS

Create a flow chart of the events that lead directly from the twins' birth to their death. You could begin it like this:

| The twins are separated | → | They meet and become friends | → | Mrs Lyons is angry | → | |

CHECKPOINT 13 (A01)

Why does Mickey come to the conclusion that Edward is the father of Linda's baby? Is his reasoning valid?

PROGRESS AND REVISION CHECK

SECTION ONE: CHECK YOUR KNOWLEDGE

Answer these quick questions to test your basic knowledge of the play, its characters and events:

1. What is the first thing shown on stage at the beginning of the play?

2. How does Russell first show Mrs Johnstone's financial problems at the beginning of the play?

3. How many children does Mrs Johnstone have after Mickey and Edward are born?

4. Why is it significant that Mr Lyons is away when Mrs Johnstone and Mrs Lyons first make their agreement?

5. How does Mrs Johnstone explain to her other children that one of the twins is missing?

6. What does Mrs Lyons give Mrs Johnstone when she sacks her?

7. What is the first thing that Edward gives Mickey?

8. What prompts Mrs Lyons to hit Edward?

9. What does the policeman say to Mrs Johnstone and Mrs Lyons when Mickey and Edward are caught throwing stones at windows?

10. What leaving present does Edward give to Mickey when they move house?

11. Why does Edward hardly ever see any girls when he is a teenager?

12. What is inside the locket that Mrs Johnstone gives to Eddie?

13. Who does Mrs Lyons first think is in the picture that she finds in Edward's locket – and why?

14. Why does Mrs Lyons attack Mrs Johnstone with a kitchen knife?

15. What is Edward talking to Linda about when Sammy is persuading Mickey to help him rob a filling station?

16. How does Mickey get a new house and a new job after he has come out of prison?

17. Where does Mickey get the gun with which he shoots Edward?

18. How does Mickey find out about Linda and Edward's affair?

19. Who shoots Mickey dead?

20. What are the two things that the Narrator suggests could be blamed for the twins' deaths?

SECTION TWO: CHECK YOUR UNDERSTANDING

Here are two tasks that require more thought and slightly longer responses. In each case, try to write at least three to four paragraphs.

Task 1: Look again at the scene in which Mrs Lyons sacks Mrs Johnstone (Act One, pp. 22–4). What is significant about this scene? Think about:

● The relationship between Mrs Johnstone and Mrs Lyons
● The impact this has on the rest of the play

Task 2: In Act Two (pp. 82–3), we see Mickey, Edward and Linda growing up. Why is this sequence important? Think about:

● What it shows the audience about the three friends
● How the plot develops after this scene

PROGRESS CHECK

GOOD PROGRESS

I can:

● understand how Russell has sequenced and revealed events. ☐
● refer to the importance of key events in the play. ☐
● select well-chosen evidence, including key quotations, to support my ideas. ☐

EXCELLENT PROGRESS

I can:

● refer in depth to main and minor events and how they contribute to the development of the plot. ☐
● understand how Russell has carefully ordered or revealed events for particular effects. ☐
● draw on a range of carefully selected key evidence, including quotations, to support my ideas. ☐

WHO'S WHO?

The Narrator

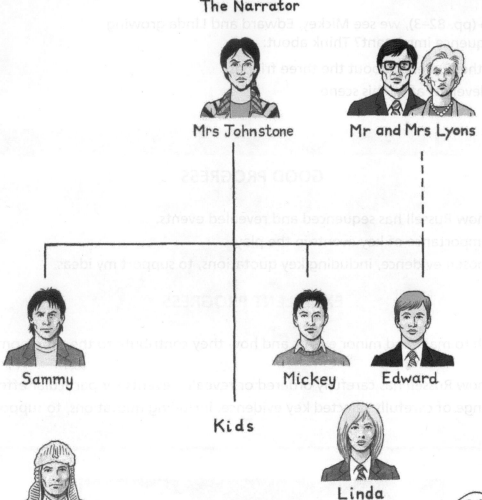

Mrs Johnstone

Mr and Mrs Lyons

Sammy

Mickey   **Edward**

Kids

The Judge

Linda

The Dole-ites

The Milkman

Policemen

Teachers

Gynaecologist

MRS JOHNSTONE

MRS JOHNSTONE'S ROLE IN THE PLAY

Mrs Johnstone is the mother of Edward and Mickey. In the play she:

- has lots of children but little money
- works as a cleaner for Mrs Lyons
- is encouraged by Mrs Lyons to give her one of her twins
- is sacked by Mrs Lyons
- gives Edward a locket containing a picture of her and Mickey
- moves house and tries to start a new life with her family
- goes to the Town Hall where Mickey is pointing a gun at Edward and tells them that they are twins.

EXAM FOCUS: WRITING ABOUT MRS JOHNSTONE

Key point	Evidence/further meaning
• She feels forced by her circumstances to give one of her twins to Mrs Lyons.	• Mrs Lyons says, 'with two more children how can you possibly avoid some of them being put into care?' (Act One, p. 12). • Mrs Johnstone thinks she is doing the best for her children.
• She gives Edward the locket which leads Mrs Lyons to discover that she is still in contact with him.	• 'I wanted him to have a picture of me' (Act Two, p. 77) • Despite her agreement with Mrs Lyons, she cannot sever her relationship with Edward. This plays a significant part in Mrs Lyons's decisions and, therefore, in the twins' deaths.
• Some of her decisions as a parent are questionable.	• 'Go on before I throw a bucket of water over the pair of y' ...' (Act Two, p. 77) • Mrs Johnstone does not object to Mickey and Edward going to watch a pornographic film. While this may appear irresponsible, it could also suggest that she understands her sons and accepts that they are growing up.

TOP TIP: VIEWS ON MRS JOHNSTONE (A01)

Think about how some of the other characters see Mrs Johnstone. How do Mrs Lyons, Edward and Mickey describe her? How and why do their views change as the story develops? Use evidence from the text to support your ideas.

MICKEY

MICKEY'S ROLE IN THE PLAY

Mickey is one of Mrs Johnstone's twins – the one she keeps. In the play, he:

- meets Edward in the street when they are both seven, and becomes his blood brother
- is suspended from school, aged fourteen
- leaves school and gets a job in a factory
- finally tells Linda how he feels about her and becomes her boyfriend
- marries Linda when they discover she is pregnant
- is made redundant
- takes part in a robbery with his brother Sammy, as a result of which he is sent to prison
- discovers Linda is having an affair with Edward
- accidentally shoots Edward dead and is shot dead by police marksmen.

EXAM FOCUS: WRITING ABOUT MICKEY

Key point	Evidence/further meaning
• Throughout the play, Russell creates parallels and contrasts between Mickey and Edward.	• 'I know loads of words like that. Y' know, like the "F" word.' (Act One, p. 28) • At the age of seven, Mickey seems far more worldly wise than naïve Edward.
• Mickey cannot bring himself to tell Linda how he feels about her.	• 'Linda, I wanna kiss y' , an' put me arms around y' ... but I don't know how to tell y' ' (Act Two, p. 71) • This suggests a shyness and vulnerability which becomes even more apparent as he fails to cope with the pressures of adult life.
• Mickey seems destroyed by his time in prison.	• 'I can't cope with this. I'm not well ... I can't do things ... Leave me alone ...' (Act Two, p. 98) • Mickey pushes Linda away, and becomes totally dependent on the pills which make him feel 'invisible' (Act Two, p. 100).

TOP TIP: CHANGES IN MICKEY (A01)

Think about the ways in which Mickey's relationship with Edward changes. As a child, Mickey seems dominant, for example taking sweets from Edward, teaching him swear words, bragging to Edward about how he was disrespectful to policemen. As an adult, however, Mickey is unable to cope, while Edward helps him, organising a new house and job for him. While Mickey seems to teach and influence Edward in childhood, Edward seems much better prepared for life as an adult.

EDWARD

EDWARD'S ROLE IN THE PLAY

Edward is the twin whom Mrs Johnstone gives to Mrs Lyons. In the play he:

- meets Mickey in the street when they are both seven and becomes his blood brother
- is told by Mrs Lyons not to see Mickey again
- is given a locket by Mrs Johnstone when he moves away
- is suspended from school when he is fourteen
- persuades Mickey to tell Linda how he feels
- goes to university
- comes home for Christmas and tells Linda he has always loved her
- becomes a local councillor and begins an affair with Linda
- is shot dead by Mickey.

EXAM FOCUS: WRITING ABOUT EDWARD

Key point	Evidence/further meaning
Edward leads a much more protected and privileged life than Mickey.	Mrs Lyons: 'I'll give you some more lessons when you're home for half term.' (Act Two, p. 61) Edward goes to boarding school and is taught how to waltz by Mrs Lyons.
In childhood, Edward's naivety makes him susceptible to Mickey's influence.	Mickey: 'when they ask what y' name is, we say things like, like "Adolf Hitler"' (Act One, p. 43) Edward believes Mickey, copies him and gets all three of them into trouble with the police.
In their teenage years and adulthood, Edward supports Mickey.	'Will you talk to Linda?' (Act Two, p. 86) It is Edward who persuades Mickey to tell Linda how he feels – despite his own feelings for her. Later, he arranges a new job and house for Mickey.

AIMING HIGH: THE PLAY'S CLIMAX

Think about the role that Edward plays in the climax of *Blood Brothers*. After going to university, he appears much less frequently on stage, appearing only once, with one line between Mickey's arrest and his death: 'Hey' (Act Two, p. 101). His affair with Linda, which is so significant to the plot, is conveyed largely visually rather than through dialogue and in the final scene he says very little. Mickey's downfall dominates and is the focus of the play's resolution. Look, for example, at the final scene (pp. 105–6): compare Mickey's dominance in this scene with Edward's responses to it.

TOP TIP A02

Compare this summary of Edward's role in the play with the summary of Mickey's role on the page opposite. How many parallels and similarities can you identify?

MRS LYONS

MRS LYONS'S ROLE IN THE PLAY

Mrs Lyons is Edward's adoptive mother. In the play she:

- lives in a large house with her husband but is childless
- persuades her cleaner, Mrs Johnstone, to give up one of her twins
- sacks Mrs Johnstone, gives her fifty pounds and tells her that the twins will die if they discover that they are brothers
- is very upset when she finds out that Mickey and Edward have been playing together
- persuades her husband that they should move to the countryside
- is disturbed when she finds out that Edward wears a locket containing a picture of Mrs Johnstone and Mickey
- tries to attack Mrs Johnston with a kitchen knife
- points out to Mickey that Edward and Linda are having an affair.

EXAM FOCUS: WRITING ABOUT MRS LYONS

Key point	Evidence/further meaning
- In her first appearance, she is presented sympathetically.	- 'we bought such a large house for the – for the children – we thought children would come along.' (Act One, p. 8) - Childless and with her husband away, Mrs Lyons seems desperate and vulnerable at the beginning of the play.
- Her manipulation of Mrs Johnstone seems calculating and heartless.	- 'You won't tell anyone about this, Mrs Johnstone, because if you do, you will kill them.' (Act One, p. 23) - Russell's language choice here – particularly 'you will kill them' – suggests that Mrs Lyons is playing on Mrs Johnstone's fears, frightening her into silence.
- Her final act in the play is to draw Mickey's attention to Linda's infidelity.	- Russell does not give Mrs Lyons dialogue at this point. She 'points out' (Act Two, p. 103) Linda and Edward to Mickey. - This final vindictive act casts her in the role of villain.

KEY QUOTATION: A CHILD OF ONE'S OWN A01

Before Edward is born, Mrs Lyons has an idealised concept of parenthood: 'I'd keep him warm in the winter / And cool when it shines. / I'd pull out his splinters / Without making him cry' (Act One, p. 14) and thinks that 'an adopted child can become one's own' (Act One, p. 8).

However, her determination to prevent any contact between Edward and his birth family seems to contradict that belief as she desperately tries to make Edward truly her 'own'. This contrast between her ideal of parenthood and the reality is, perhaps, what drives her to the bitter revenge of pointing out Edward and Linda's affair to Mickey.

MR LYONS

MR LYONS'S ROLE IN THE PLAY

Mr Lyons is Mrs Lyons's husband and he believes he is Edward's father. In the play he:

- is away on business at the start of the play so he believes Edward to be his own son
- is persuaded by Mrs Lyons that they should sack Mrs Johnstone
- often has to leave his wife and son to go to work
- gives Edward a toy gun
- tries to calm his wife when she is worried that Edward has disappeared; he thinks she should see a doctor
- is managing director of a local factory, and makes many of his workers redundant, including Mickey.

EXAM FOCUS: WRITING ABOUT MR LYONS (A01)

Key point	Evidence/further meaning
● Mr Lyons plays a minor role in bringing up Edward.	● 'The house is your domain. Look, Jen, I've got a board meeting. I really must dash.' (Act One, p. 21) ● Despite the lifestyle that he provides for Mrs Lyons and Edward, he makes little contribution to their emotional well-being.
● Mr Lyons is concerned about his wife's mental health.	● 'It's this depression thing that happens after a woman's had a … .' (Act One, p. 21) ● Mr Lyons assumes that Mrs Lyons's erratic behaviour is caused by post-natal depression. **Ironically** this highlights Mrs Lyons's deception of her husband.
● Mr Lyons sings cheerfully about laying off large numbers of his workforce.	● 'I'm afraid we must fire you, / We no longer require you,' (Act Two, p. 89) ● This seems to mirror Mrs Lyons's heartless attitude when she sacks Mrs Johnstone.

AIMING HIGH: THE SIGNIFICANCE OF MR LYONS ⭐

Mr Lyons makes few appearances on stage, but that is what makes him significant. This is partly a requirement of the plot: he cannot pay too much attention to his wife's pregnancy, or her deteriorating mental health, without affecting the development of the plot. It also places responsibility for Edward firmly with Mrs Lyons, giving Russell more scope to present her as controlling and overbearing. There is, however, no suggestion that Edward feels ignored or rejected by his father. Perhaps Russell is more interested in focusing on the interaction between sons and mothers.

TOP TIP (A01)

Mr Lyons is the only 'father figure' in the play. What does this suggest about Russell's view of the role of fathers?

LINDA

LINDA'S ROLE IN THE PLAY

Linda is Mickey and Edward's friend from childhood. In the play she:

● plays with Mickey and Edward when they are seven
● repeatedly tells Mickey that she loves him
● supports Mickey on the school bus and when he is suspended
● becomes Mickey's girlfriend and then marries him when they discover she is pregnant
● asks Edward to help her get a new house and a job for Mickey
● encourages Mickey to tackle his addiction
● has an affair with Edward.

EXAM FOCUS: WRITING ABOUT LINDA

Key point	Evidence/further meaning
● Linda comes from a similar background to Mickey.	● 'An' listen, Mickey, if y' dead, there's no school, is there?' (Act One, p. 42) ● Russell's use of dialect and abbreviation to reflect Linda's accent follows the same patterns as Mickey's dialogue.
● She is a strong, resourceful and independent woman.	● 'You stay where y' are, Mickey.' (Act Two, p. 64) ● For the majority of the play, Linda supports and sometimes directs Mickey's choices and actions.
● Her affair with Edward could suggest a selfish side to Linda.	● Mrs Johnstone: 'Nothing cruel, / Nothing wrong. / It's just two fools, / Who know the rules, / But break them all,' (Act Two, p. 102) ● It seems callous of Linda to abandon Mickey when he is at his lowest point. However, through Mrs Johnstone's song, Russell suggests that the audience should not condemn Edward or Linda for their affair. It is circumstance that has driven Linda away from Mickey.

TOP TIP: LINDA AND MICKEY

Russell presents Linda as a natural match for Mickey: they come from similar backgrounds; they are friends before Edward joins them; they play together as children. She consistently stands up for Mickey, for example when they play with Sammy's gang. Russell creates tension in their relationship as Mickey is unable to express his feelings – and humour when that tension is resolved in their marriage, although this is partly forced by conventional attitudes of the time to pregnancy. However, the subsequent failure of their relationship is more than a contributing factor to Mickey's downfall – it is a key part of it.

SAMMY

SAMMY'S ROLE IN THE PLAY

Sammy is Mickey's older brother. Mickey admires him and is ultimately led into criminal activity by him. In the play he:

- plays shooting games – and falls out – with Mickey, Linda and Edward
- owns the airgun that Mickey, Edward and Linda fire at the statue in the park
- burns his school down
- is chased by the police when he pulls a knife on the bus conductor
- persuades Mickey to take part in the filling station robbery
- shoots someone during the robbery.

EXAM FOCUS: WRITING ABOUT SAMMY

Key point	Evidence/further meaning
• Russell uses Sammy to highlight the most apparent difference between Mickey and Edward.	• 'He's a … poshy.' (Act One, p. 31) • While Mickey and Edward focus on their similarities, Sammy mocks Edward and his accent.
• Sammy's apparent access to guns is highly significant to the plot.	• Mickey shoots Edward with Sammy's gun which was hidden under a floorboard after the filling station robbery.
• Russell uses the character of Sammy to reflect the situation in which Mickey grows up and the choices available to him.	• 'Sammy, tell him, tell him you're really sixteen. I'll lend you the rest of the fare …' (Act Two, p. 64) • In the incident on the bus, Mickey makes the right choices and supports his brother. However, circumstances force him to make very different choices later in the play.

TOP TIP: SAMMY'S INFLUENCE OVER MICKEY (A01)

Mickey's first appearance in the play is when he sings about his admiration for Sammy: 'I wish I was our Sammy' (Act One, p. 26). His youthful enthusiasm for Sammy's wrongdoing creates humour in the first part of the play – he can 'spit / Straight in y' eye from twenty yards' (Act One, p. 26) and he 'wees straight through the letter box / Of the house next door to us' (Act One, p. 27). However, this influence takes a much more sinister turn as we see Sammy's behaviour deteriorate, burning down his school and threatening the bus conductor with a knife. Ultimately it is Sammy's influence over Mickey that results in his prison sentence.

THE NARRATOR

THE NARRATOR'S ROLE IN THE PLAY

The Narrator performs a number of different functions. In the play he:

- introduces the story of the play and reveals its ending in the first few moments
- summarises and explains the plot throughout the play
- is able, as an omniscient narrator, to remind the audience of the play's inevitable ending throughout
- remains detached from the action of the play as 'Narrator' but sometimes steps into the action, taking on a variety of minor roles, for example the Milkman and the Gynaecologist. (The director of the play may decide that the Narrator also takes on other minor roles, such as the Judge or the Policeman.)

EXAM FOCUS: WRITING ABOUT THE NARRATOR

Key point	Evidence/further meaning
He invites the audience to judge Mrs Johnstone at the start of the play.	'judge for yourselves / How she came to play this part.' (Act One, p. 5) The Narrator suggests that society has judged Mrs Johnstone 'cruel' (Act One, p. 5) but that the play will present another side of her story.
His song of superstition and impending doom recurs throughout the play.	'y' know the devil's got your number, / He's gonna find y' ' (Act One, p. 24) Like a tolling bell, the repetition of the song presents the fate of Mickey and Edward as their inevitable destiny.
He invites the audience to judge what led to the deaths of Mickey and Edward.	'And do we blame superstition for what came to pass? / Or could it be what we, the English, have come to know as class?' (Act Two, p. 107) Despite his frequent references to superstition, the Narrator casts doubt here, directly addressing the audience to suggest that Mickey and Edward's different social classes led to their deaths.

TOP TIP: THE NARRATOR'S KEY FUNCTIONS A01

The role of the Narrator can depend on the way in which it is performed: he can appear to be a powerful, almost supernatural figure, leading the characters to their fate – or a more detached storyteller, recounting events and reminding the audience that this is a 'story' (Act One, p. 5).

However the part is played, one of the Narrator's key functions is to remind the audience that every decision the characters take leads them closer to the ending that he reveals at the beginning. In this sense, he makes a significant contribution to the dramatic tension of the play.

MINOR CHARACTERS

THE MILKMAN AND GYNAECOLOGIST

Russell uses the Milkman to highlight Mrs Johnstone's financial situation at the start of the play: she cannot afford milk for her many children. The **Finance Man** and the **Catalogue Man** perform a similar role. It is also significant that, at the start of Act Two, Mrs Johnstone is up to date with payments to her new milkman and even goes dancing with him, suggesting that she has succeeded in making a new start.

The Milkman transforms into the Gynaecologist who tells Mrs Johnstone that she is having twins. The Gynaecologist says he has 'given up the milk round and gone into medicine' (Act One, p. 10) – but he delivers news which only makes Mrs Johnstone's situation worse.

POLICEMEN

The police make various appearances, most dramatically in the final scene. The policeman is used to highlight different approaches to the middle and working classes: when he catches the twins throwing stones, he threatens Mrs Johnstone with court but only suggests Mrs Lyons reduces Edward's pocket money and keeps him away from boys like Mickey.

TOP TIP (A01)

Many of the play's minor characters are figures in authority who affect and, in some cases, control elements of the character's lives.

TEACHERS

The teachers – possibly played by the same actor – might be considered typical of their schools: Edward's boarding school and Mickey's secondary modern. They suspend the boys for relatively minor misdemeanours.

THE JUDGE

The Judge is presented humorously, giving Sammy a lighter sentence because he is attracted to Mrs Johnstone. Again, Russell creates an authority figure whose actions and decisions are far from impartial.

KIDS AND DOLE-ITES

Mrs Johnstone's many children often speak from 'off stage', demanding food or items from 'the catalogue' (Act One, p. 19). Mrs Johnstone agrees to their demands, suggesting that she is loving but financially irresponsible.

The queue of Dole-ites is created from the guests at Mickey and Linda's wedding, indicating that the happiness of the wedding will soon be overtaken by the misery of Mickey's redundancy.

KEY CONTEXT (A03)

The Dole-ites draw attention to issues of mass unemployment in the 1980s.

PROGRESS AND REVISION CHECK

TOP TIP **(A01)**

Answer these quick questions to test your basic knowledge of the play's characters.

SECTION ONE: CHECK YOUR KNOWLEDGE

1. Why does Mrs Johnstone give Edward her locket?
2. Note down one thing that Edward admires about Mickey when they are seven.
3. How does Edward help Mickey when they are teenagers?
4. Note down one incident which reveals to Mrs Lyons, and to the audience, the influence that Mickey has on Edward when they are children.
5. What are the three things Sammy does that get him into trouble with the police.
6. Note down one instance where Linda supports Mickey.
7. How does Russell create sympathy for Mrs Lyons?
8. How does Mr Lyons show some concern for his wife?
9. Note down one other role which the Narrator takes on in the play.
10. In what ways are Mickey's and Edward's teachers similar?

TOP TIP **(A01)**

This task requires more thought and a slightly longer response. Try to write at least three to four paragraphs.

SECTION TWO: CHECK YOUR UNDERSTANDING

Task: How does Russell present Mrs Johnstone through:

- the decisions she makes
- other characters' interactions with and responses to her?

PROGRESS CHECK

GOOD PROGRESS

I can:

- explain the significance of the main characters in how the action develops. ☐
- refer to how they are presented by Russell and how this affects the way we see them. ☐

EXCELLENT PROGRESS

I can:

- analyse in detail how Russell has shaped and developed characters over the course of the play. ☐
- infer key ideas, themes and issues from the ways characters and relationships are presented by Russell. ☐

THEMES

CLASS

At the end of the play, the Narrator suggests that 'class' could be blamed for 'what came to pass' (Act Two, p. 107). It is clearly one of the key differences in the lives of Mickey and Edward.

There are some very obvious class differences between the two when they first meet, aged seven:

- Edward speaks in standard English, using stereotypically middle class language, while working class Mickey uses dialect, slang and swear words, and speaks in a Liverpudlian accent:

  > **Mickey** ... if our Sammy gives y' a sweet he's usually weed on it first.
  > **Edward** *(exploding in giggles)* Oh, that sounds like super fun.
  > (Act One, p. 28)

- Edward's reference to, and Mickey's ignorance of, 'The dictionary' (Act One, p. 29) suggests that they and their parents have very different attitudes to books and education. This becomes more apparent when Edward is sent to a private, single-sex boarding school while Mickey goes to the local secondary modern school.

- Money is an important element of class: Mr and Mrs Lyons have a great deal of it – they live in a large house and employ a cleaner – while Mrs Johnstone cannot pay the Milkman.

TOP TIP: WRITING ABOUT CLASS (A01)

Russell emphasises that the twins' differing social class has more significant consequences than their wealth or their accents or attitudes. The key difference between the twins, which only becomes apparent as they reach adulthood, is the opportunities and choices they have: Edward is able to go to university and become a local councillor; Mickey is at the mercy of his employer – Edward's father. On being made redundant, Mickey resorts to crime and is imprisoned. On his release from prison he is unable to cope and so Linda resorts to seeking Edward's help.

The overall impression Russell creates is of a helpless and vulnerable working class at the mercy of, and ultimately reliant on, a largely uncaring middle class.

THEME TRACKER (A01)

Class

- Act One, p. 37: Mrs Lyons is appalled at the 'filth' that Edward has learnt from 'horrible' boys like Mickey.

- Act One, pp. 47–8: The Policeman reports different accounts of Mickey's and Edward's behaviour, and suggests different punishments to their mothers. This seems to suggest that the police treat the working and middle classes differently.

- Act Two, pp. 95–6: While Edward celebrates Christmas with his university friends, Mickey robs a filling station with his older brother Sammy.

AIMING HIGH: NATURE AND NURTURE

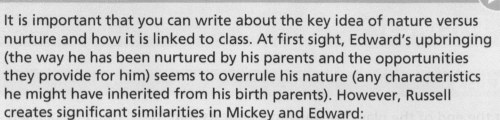

It is important that you can write about the key idea of nature versus nurture and how it is linked to class. At first sight, Edward's upbringing (the way he has been nurtured by his parents and the opportunities they provide for him) seems to overrule his nature (any characteristics he might have inherited from his birth parents). However, Russell creates significant similarities in Mickey and Edward:

- They both swear.
- They both play with guns.
- They are both suspended.
- They are both attracted to Linda.

Does this suggest that sometimes Edward's true Johnstone nature shows through his parents' efforts to make him their own? Or are these simply qualities and incidents which could be applied to anyone of any class? Edward is clearly drawn to the Johnstone family – but perhaps they offer the kind of affection and freedom that is lacking in his own home.

THEME TRACKER (A01)

Parents and children

- Act One, pp. 12–14: Mrs Johnstone and Mrs Lyons sing about their hopes for Edward.

- Act Two, pp. 60–1: Mrs Johnstone laughs about Mickey's interest in girls; Mrs Lyons is teaching Edward to waltz while he complains that he never meets any girls.

- Act Two, p. 77: Edward thinks Mrs Johnstone is 'fabulous' when she laughs at them for going to see *Nymphomaniac Nights* and *Swedish Au Pairs*.

PARENTS AND CHILDREN

Mrs Johnstone's and Mrs Lyons's approaches to parenting are very different:

- Mrs Johnstone allows her children freedom: she laughs when she works out that the twins are going to see *Nymphomaniac Nights* and *Swedish Au Pairs* and makes excuses for Sammy when he burns the school down, blaming the teacher because he lets them 'Play with magnesium' (Act Two, p. 59).

- While it could be argued that she allows them too much freedom, she does impose some rules; for example, Mickey complains about all the things he is not allowed to do because he is only seven: he's not allowed to 'go to the baths' and he has to go bed 'at seven' (Act One, p. 26).

- Mrs Lyons, though, is much stricter and more controlling, for example, attempting to confine Edward to the garden to play on his own while Mickey and his friends play in the street. All her decisions seem driven by the need to keep Edward away from Mickey, although she tells him that 'It's only because I love you, Edward.' (Act One, p. 36).

TOP TIP: COMPARING HOMES (A02)

Note how Russell presents two very different images of the Lyons and Johnstone households. Mrs Johnstone's home is presented as loving but chaotic, dominated by children demanding 'Meccano ... a new dress ... an air pistol' (Act One, p. 19). In contrast, the Lyons family is presented as a model middle class family group: Edward and his father 'romp on the floor' (Act One, p. 34), his father gives him a toy gun, and Mrs Lyons reads him a story. This idyllic picture of family bliss is soon shattered: Mr Lyons has to go back to work; Mickey knocks on the door and, when he has gone, Mrs Lyons argues with Edward and hits him for swearing at her. Neither home is presented as perfect.

GROWING UP

The play shows key points in Mickey and Edward's childhood:

- They play games with guns and get in trouble with the police when they are seven.
- They are both suspended from school when they are fourteen, watch a pornographic film at the cinema, agonise over girls, go to the fair and to the beach with Linda, are disrespectful to a policeman and run away.

Up to this point, the twins seem inseparable – the huge difference in their home lives, moving house, and even Mrs Lyons's attempts to separate them, seem unable to come between Mickey and Edward.

However, this all changes at the pivotal point in the play when Edward returns from university for Christmas to discover that Linda is pregnant and married to Mickey:

- While Mickey has been thrown suddenly and sharply into a world of adult responsibilities, Edward is still in a teenage world of parties and friends, as Mickey points out with bitter resentment: 'you're still a kid. An' I wish I could be as well, Eddie, I wish I could still believe in all that blood brother stuff. But I can't, because while no one was looking I grew up' (Act Two, p. 92).
- In response, Edward says nothing; he simply 'backs away' (Act Two, p. 93). After eighteen years, it seems the bond between the twins is finally broken by the demands of adulthood.

AIMING HIGH: SEEDS OF CHANGE ⭐

The changes in the twins as they grow, and their changing relationship, strongly suggests how they grow apart as they grow up – and how the values and qualities that children have are very different from those needed in adult life.

However, it could be argued that Russell plants the seeds of the twins' conflict from their earliest appearance in the play. When Mickey and Edward are seven, Edward admires Mickey's language, his stories, his brother's gun, and his attitude to the police. Some of these are reflected in the values that dominate Mickey's adult life: in particular his relationship with his brother Sammy, and his attitude to criminal behaviour. To an extent, the seeds of Mickey's downfall, and the ultimate destruction of the twins and their relationship, can be seen in the behaviour  of the seven-year-old Mickey that Edward once so admired. The limits of Mickey's antisocial behaviour were once an ambition to urinate through a letter box like his brother Sammy, but in adult life he takes part in armed robberies with him. Where once Edward looked up rude words in the dictionary, in adult life he uses his intellect to go to university and become a councillor.

THEME TRACKER (A01)

Growing up

- Act One, pp. 26–9: Mickey sings about the problems of being seven; Edward is hugely impressed by Mickey.
- Act Two, pp. 71–2: Aged fourteen, Mickey and Edward sing, individually, about their teenage insecurities, and their jealousy of a boy that they see in the distance – ironically their twin.
- Act Two, p. 90–4: Edward returns from university to find that everything has changed: Linda is pregnant and married to Mickey; Mickey has taken on all the responsibilities of adulthood.

FRIENDSHIP AND BROTHERHOOD

The theme of friendship is strongly linked with the theme of growing up. Mickey and Edward's friendship is, however, more than an ordinary friendship. Though they are not aware of it, their relationship is one of brotherhood:

● Russell carefully shows the values and interests that they share in childhood and their teenage years: swearing, guns, challenging authority, romantic relationships.

● They seal their friendship within minutes of meeting with the 'blood brothers' ritual, ironically trying to become what they already are: brothers. However, as the play's resolution depends upon it, there is nothing in their relationship to suggest actual brotherhood to the brothers themselves; they do not recognise any physical similarity in each other, for example. It is precisely this that makes the play so poignant, however.

While Mickey and Edward's friendship is secure, the audience is presented with a model of brotherhood in which each supports the other. When their friendship fails, the impact is far greater for the audience because it is not just a failed friendship: it is a breakdown of brotherhood.

Perhaps the most significant example of their friendship is in their relationship with Linda. While Mickey cannot express his feelings for Linda, Edward does not take advantage of the situation; he hides his own feelings for her. It is, therefore, yet more significant that it is Linda and Edward's affair that brings the breakdown of their relationship to a head, symbolising the breaking of their bond.

TOP TIP: WRITING ABOUT FRIENDSHIP (A01)

Consider the values of friendship that Russell presents in the play. These are clear in the twins' childhood and teenage years. However, under the pressures of adulthood, Mickey dismisses their friendship as 'kids' stuff' (Act Two, p. 93) and pushes Edward away. Edward's affair with Linda could be seen as a kind of retaliation – or perhaps something he feels only able to do once their friendship has ended – or perhaps it allows Russell to balance the blame between the two twins: should both of them take some responsibility for the breakdown of their relationship and subsequent death?

FATE AND SUPERSTITION

The Narrator's references to superstition throughout the play ensure it remains constantly in the audience's minds:

- Initially, Russell uses Mrs Johnstone's superstition to reveal Mrs Lyons's manipulation of her. Mrs Lyons warns Mrs Johnstone: 'You do know what they say about twins, secretly parted, don't you?' (Act One, p. 23).
- This also allows Russell to use Mrs Johnstone's belief in superstition to ensure her silence about the twins' identity, until the play's dramatic conclusion.

There are other ways Russell uses superstition in the play too:

- He uses superstition to show Mickey's enduring influence over Edward, even after the Lyons family have moved away. Edward is upset to see a magpie which he believes brings 'sorrow' because 'Mickey told me' (Act One, p. 52).
- Russell uses superstition to suggest Mrs Lyons's mental fragility: at the start of the play, Mrs Lyons laughs at Mrs Johnstone's superstition about putting shoes on a table; towards the end of Act One, she herself 'sweeps' a pair of shoes from a table, placed there by Mr Lyons, who has just suggested that she 'should see a doctor' (Act One, p. 45).

Each subsequent reference by the Narrator then reminds the audience of the ending which they have been shown in the opening moments of the play. Russell uses superstition and the twins' certain fate to build dramatic tension as the play progresses to its inevitable, tragic conclusion: 'the devil's got your number ... / he's callin' your number up today / Today / Today / TODAY!' (Act Two, p. 104).

AIMING HIGH: SUPERSTITION AND CLASS

Does Russell believe in superstition? At the end of the play, the Narrator undermines the significance of every reference to superstition in the play: 'And do we blame superstition for what came to pass? / Or could it be what we, the English, have come to know as class?' (Act Two, p. 107). This strongly suggests that Russell has simply used superstition and fate for dramatic purposes: to reveal character and character development, to suggest the influence of characters over each other, and, above all, to manipulate the audience's response to the events depicted on stage. Perhaps, though, he suggests in Mrs Johnstone's initial belief, and in Mrs Lyons's conversion to superstition, that we can all be brought to believe in things which provide a degree of certainty and inevitability when facing an uncertain and difficult future.

THEME TRACKER (A01)

Fate and superstition

- Act One, p. 23: Mrs Lyons warns Mrs Johnstone about the superstition of separating twins.
- Act One, p. 45: Mrs Lyons becomes superstitious, frightened to find a pair of shoes on her table.
- Throughout Act One and Two: The Narrator reminds the audience of the power of superstition.

KEY CONTEXT (A03)

A tragedy is not simply a story which ends unhappily: the key feature which defines the tragic form in drama is that it focuses on a 'hero' whose downfall and death are the inevitable and unavoidable consequence of a flaw in their character or their circumstances. In *Blood Brothers*, Mickey and Edward are the focus of the play's tragedy: their tragic downfall is the result of circumstances which they neither know about nor can control.

CONTEXTS

WILLY RUSSELL'S LIFE

Willy Russell was born in 1947 in Whiston, just outside Liverpool, in a traditionally working class household. His father had a number of jobs: in the mining industry, in a factory, in a fish and chip shop. His mother was a nurse and later worked in a warehouse. He left school at the age of fifteen with just one O'level: a D in English Language. He was initially a ladies' hairdresser, then went to evening classes and university, and eventually became a teacher. Russell has written a number of other successful plays and film scripts, including *Educating Rita* and *Shirley Valentine.*

WHEN IS THE PLAY SET?

The time period in which *Blood Brothers* is set is not explicitly referred to in the play. However, there are clues:

● References to Marilyn Monroe suggest the twins are born in the 1950s.

● The Lyons and the Johnstone families move to Skelmersdale at the end of Act One, as many people from Liverpool did in the 1960s.

● The economic situation at the end of the play suggests the early 1980s, when the play was written.

AIMING HIGH: MRS JOHNSTONE AND MARILYN MONROE

There are a number of significant references in the play to Marilyn Monroe, the actress and film star who epitomised glamour and sexuality but died of a drugs overdose in 1963. Most of these references are made by Mrs Johnstone.

● The first is when describing her relationship with her husband.

● At the beginning of Act Two, she says her new boyfriend, Joe, has compared her to Marilyn.

● Towards the end of Act Two she compares Mickey's addiction to Marilyn Monroe's.

These references to the romance and glamour of Hollywood – and the reality behind it – create a stark comparison between Mrs Johnstone's romanticised hopes of a Hollywood ending and the reality that she must actually face.

TOP TIP: WRITING ABOUT RUSSELL'S LIFE (A03)

Some of the key themes that Russell explores in his writing are reflected in his own experience, notably that of growing up in a working class family and the value of education in transforming lives. Make sure you draw links to evidence in the play when writing about Russell's own life and experiences.

BRITAIN IN THE 1980S

In 1981, when the play was completed, Margaret Thatcher had been the British prime minister for two years. Under her leadership, the Conservative party reduced the power of the trade unions in the hope of making British industry more competitive. This particularly affected cities that relied on their manufacturing industries, including Liverpool. One result was a huge rise in unemployment which had, in turn, significant impacts on the lives of the people who lived there: poverty, crime and drug abuse increased dramatically. Russell clearly highlights these impacts of unemployment in the fate of Mickey in *Blood Brothers*.

Margaret Thatcher once said in an interview: 'I do not know anyone who has got to the top without hard work. That is the recipe. It will not always get you to the top, but it should get you pretty near.' However, Russell challenges this belief in *Blood Brothers*: it is not hard work that makes Mickey and Edward's lives so different; it is the opportunities that their backgrounds provide for them.

EDUCATION AND CAREERS

Mickey and Edward's differing educations reveal as much as, if not more than, anything else about the great divide between the twins' lives. As a result of the Education Act of 1944, secondary state schools in many areas became either 'secondary modern' schools or 'grammar' schools. Students took an exam at the end of primary school which assessed their academic ability: the top 20 per cent went to a grammar school, the rest to a secondary modern. Grammar schools taught a highly academic curriculum while secondary modern schools in some areas taught more practical subjects, aiming to prepare students for more administrative or manual jobs, or for looking after the home.

Many people supported this development, believing it would help social mobility, allowing the most academic students to flourish, regardless of their social background. While they were intended to be equally valued, in practice, grammar schools received much more funding and secondary moderns came to be seen as 'sink' schools. Mickey might be regarded as a typical secondary modern student.

In the 1960s, when Mickey and Edward would have been at school, around seven per cent of students were educated in private, fee-paying schools, like Edward's boarding school. The average boarding school fees in the 1960s would have been approximately 25 per cent of the average wage and were therefore only affordable for those earning considerably more than the average.

REVISION FOCUS: THE RELEVANCE OF CONTEXT

To help you consider the relevance of context in the play, make notes on all the differences in Mickey and Edward's lives as well the similarities: their education, their financial situation, their family situation; and the advantages and disadvantages that these bring.

KEY CONTEXT

One of the key roles of a trade union is to protect the interests of its members. Before the Thatcher government, the unions were much more powerful and would go on strike if an employer tried to make any of their members redundant. When Thatcher reduced the unions' power, employers were able to make their workers redundant much more easily – just as Mr Lyons makes Mickey redundant in *Blood Brothers*.

SETTINGS

TWO HOUSES

There should be no 'cumbersome scene changes' (p. 2) in the play, according to the Production note which precedes the script. Although the action moves from Liverpool to Skelmersdale in Act Two, the set remains unchanged: the audience sees two houses, the Lyons's and Mrs Johnstone's. Scenes take place inside Mrs Lyons's house, but the interior of Mrs Johnstone's is not seen.

There are, however, very few significant references to the two houses or the differences between them in the script. Mrs Lyons's house is 'large' and 'pretty' and so 'lovely' that Mrs Johnstone thinks it's 'a pleasure to clean it' (Act One, p. 8). No information is given as to the size, style or standard of the Johnstone's house. However, Mrs Johnstone gives some sense of the range of people living in their area of Liverpool. Mrs Johnstone warns Mickey not to play with 'those hooligans down at the rough end' (Act One, p. 25). Mickey explains that they are playing at 'the other end', near where the Lyons family live in one of the 'big houses in the park' (Act One, p. 25). The idea of 'big houses' set in a 'park' certainly suggests the affluence of the Lyons's house and its location in comparison to Mrs Johnstone's.

NEW TOWN, NEW LIFE?

The Lyons family move house in order to move away from Mickey and Mrs Johnstone – who, ironically, also wants to move in order to start again, to 'Where nobody's heard of our name' (Act One, p. 57). Russell paints a picture of the 'muck an' the dirt an' the ... trouble' (Act One, p. 57) of Liverpool that Mrs Johnstone wants to escape, and her happiness at the rural life of Skelmersdale which Mickey thinks is 'like the country', with fields and cows, one of which she has to tell Sammy to 'Get off' before pointing out that 'that cow's a bull' (Act One, p. 57).

Although the settings help to ground the play, neither family can escape their past by moving house: both take their worries and problems with them. In the first minute of Act Two, Mrs Johnstone reveals that Sammy has been arrested for burning down his school – and Mrs Lyons soon discovers that not only has Edward been in touch with Mickey and Mrs Johnstone, but they have followed her to Skelmersdale.

LIVERPOOL

The Johnstones' house

The Lyons's house

PARK

SKELMERSDALE

The Johnstones' house

The Lyons's house

PROGRESS AND REVISION CHECK

SECTION ONE: CHECK YOUR KNOWLEDGE

1. Write down three ways in which Edward's life seems more privileged than Mickey's.

2. When does Mickey and Edward's friendship start to disintegrate?

3. How does Mrs Lyons's attitude to superstition change during the play?

4. Choose two words or phrases to describe Mrs Lyons and Mrs Johnstone's different styles of parenting.

5. What does the Narrator, at the end of the play, suggest might have caused the deaths of the twins?

6. What were some of the consequences of unemployment in Liverpool in the 1980s?

7. Who was Marilyn Monroe?

8. Where and when is the play set?

9. What does Sammy get told off for doing when the Johnstones first arrive in Skelmersdale?

10. Where in Liverpool is the Lyons's house?

SECTION TWO: CHECK YOUR UNDERSTANDING

Task: How does Russell show the differences between Mickey and Edward? Think about:

● What the events and setting of the play suggest about their lives
● How Russell uses their differences to explore key themes and ideas

PROGRESS CHECK

GOOD PROGRESS

I can:

● explain the main themes, contexts and settings in the text and how they contribute to the effect on the audience. ☐
● use a range of appropriate evidence to support any points I make about these elements. ☐

EXCELLENT PROGRESS

I can:

● analyse in detail the way themes are developed and presented across the play. ☐
● refer closely to key aspects of context and setting and the implications they have for the writer's viewpoint, and the interpretation of relationships and ideas. ☐

FORM

A PLAY WITH MUSIC

Blood Brothers has been described as a 'musical' and as a 'play with music'. Its songs allow the characters to express their inner thoughts and feelings – much like soliloquys in conventional drama. However, the events depicted in *Blood Brothers* are largely played out through the spoken word, rather than through song.

TRAGEDY

The definition of tragedy can vary. Key elements of the genre usually include a hero who, through a flaw in their personality or because of an error of judgement, meets their inevitable doom. In Shakespearian tragedy, the hero is often a high status character who loses everything, largely through their own flawed choices, while the decisions or actions of other characters also contribute to their suffering.

In *Blood Brothers*, Mickey and Edward seem to display some of the features of tragic heroes: they certainly meet an unhappy end which Russell presents as inevitable by revealing it at the start of the play. At almost precisely halfway through Act Two Mickey has a best friend and a job, he gets married and is going to have a baby; by the end of the play he is addicted to pills; has lost his best friend, his job and his wife; and believes Edward may be the father of his child. In that sense, the tragedy of *Blood Brothers* is very much Mickey's tragedy – and, just as they shared everything throughout their childhood, he shares it with his twin, killing Edward before he is shot himself.

In one sense, Russell presents their tragic end as the inevitable consequence of decisions taken by Mrs Johnstone and Mrs Lyons when the twins were born. It could be suggested that Mrs Johnstone's poverty and Mrs Lyons's desperate jealousy are the personality flaws that spark the inevitable tragedy. However, Mickey and Edward's own decisions contribute to their end: Mickey's decision to join Sammy in the robbery, and Edward's decision to have an affair with Linda. Ultimately, Russell suggests, through the Narrator, that it is 'class' (Act Two, p. 107) which causes their downfall: the society in which they grew up.

REVISION FOCUS: COMPARING TRAGEDIES

Try comparing *Blood Brothers* with another tragedy you have studied, for example, Shakespeare's *Macbeth* or *Romeo and Juliet*. What elements of tragedy do they have in common? How do they differ?

TOP TIP A02

Think carefully about the songs that specific characters sing and which recur at various points in the play. For example, Mrs Johnstone sings a single line of a song at the very opening of the play and sings the same song in full at the end of the play, linking the beginning and the ending of the play, in the same way as the Narrator does.

TOP TIP (A02)

Use your revision to make sure you are very clear on the parallels and contrasts in *Blood Brothers*: they are a key structural element of the play.

STRUCTURE

PARALLELS AND CONTRASTS

The plot of *Blood Brothers*, and its impact on an audience, is strengthened through the web of parallels and contrasts created by Willy Russell.

Parallels encourage the audience to compare characters.
Contrasts emphasise their very significant differences.

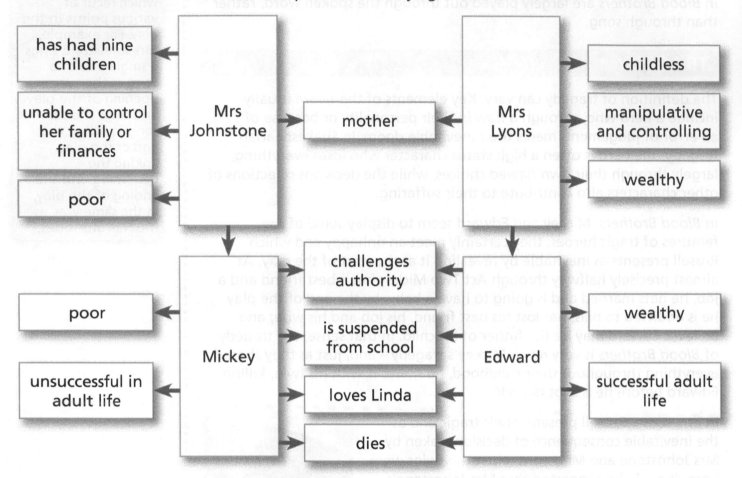

Mrs Johnstone		Mrs Lyons
has had nine children	mother	childless
unable to control her family or finances		manipulative and controlling
poor		wealthy

Mickey		Edward
poor	challenges authority	wealthy
	is suspended from school	
unsuccessful in adult life	loves Linda	successful adult life
	dies	

THE RISE AND FALL OF THE PLOT

The plot is a key factor in the engagement and interest of the reader or audience in any text. Russell maintains his audience's engagement, firstly through the trials and tribulations of Mrs Johnstone and Mrs Lyons but ultimately through those of Mickey and Edward.

Mickey and Edward spend the first three-quarters of the play – up until the second half of Act Two – cementing their blood brother bond. Prior to that point, it seems that the workings of fate, superstition and Mrs Lyons cannot separate them or break their friendship. Hopes are raised that they might somehow cheat their fate.

However, in the second half of Act Two, despite the promise of a happy ending in the form of a loving marriage and a new baby, Mickey's fortunes take a downward turn: unemployment, a broken friendship, crime, prison, drugs and an affair all conspire to bring the twins to their tragic fate. The rise and fall of the plot is shown in the diagram on the opposite page.

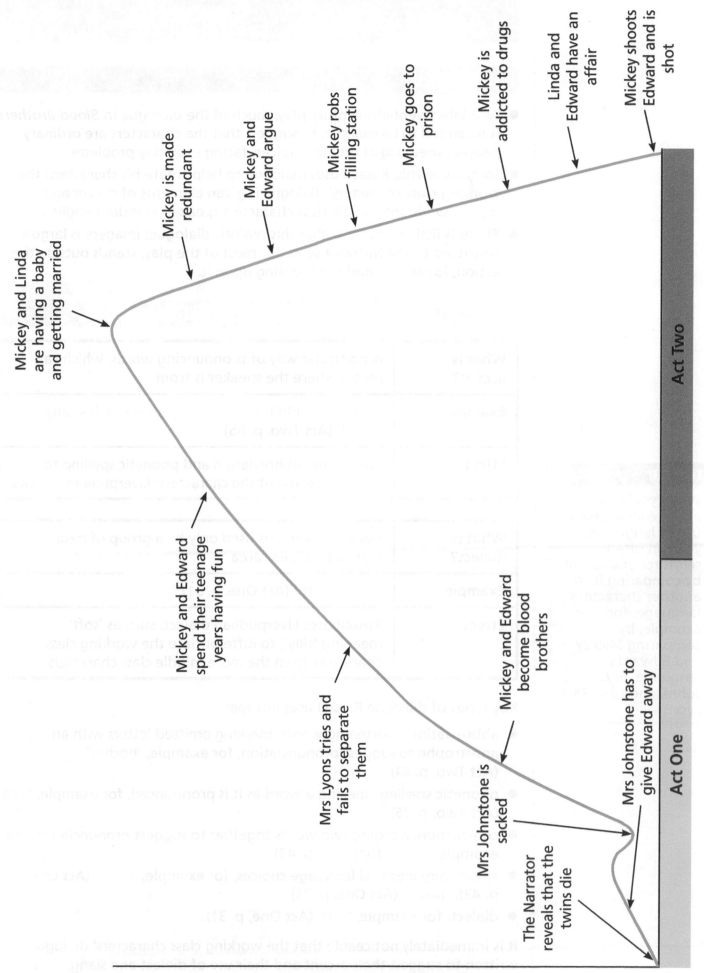

Chance of a happy ending

Mickey and Linda are having a baby and getting married

Mickey is made redundant

Mickey and Edward argue

Mickey robs filling station

Mickey goes to prison

Mickey is addicted to drugs

Linda and Edward have an affair

Mickey shoots Edward and is shot

Mickey and Edward spend their teenage years having fun

Mrs Lyons tries and fails to separate them

Mickey and Edward become blood brothers

Mrs Johnstone is sacked

Mrs Johnstone has to give Edward away

The Narrator reveals that the twins die

Act One

Act Two

LANGUAGE

OVERVIEW

- As a late twentieth-century play, much of the dialogue in *Blood Brothers* is intended to be realistic, to suggest that the characters are ordinary people, speaking in ordinary voices, facing everyday problems.
- To achieve this, Russell uses dialogue to help create his characters: the working class characters' dialogue is given elements of accent and dialect while the middle class characters speak in standard English.
- There is little imagery within this realistic dialogue; imagery is largely restricted to the Narrator who, for most of the play, stands outside the action, looking in and commenting upon it.

LANGUAGE DEVICE: ACCENT AND DIALECT

What is accent?	A particular way of pronouncing words, which can reveal where the speaker is from
Example	'Y' better hadn't or I won't be in love with y' any more!' (Act Two, p. 65)
Effect	Russell uses abbreviation and phonetic spelling to represent some of the characters' Liverpudlian accents.

What is dialect?	Vocabulary that is used only by a group of people from a particular area
Example	'You're soft.' (Act One, p. 31)
Effect	Russell uses Liverpudlian dialect, such as 'soft' meaning 'silly', to differentiate the working class characters from the more middle class characters.

Key types of dialogue Russell uses include:

- abbreviation: shortening words, marking omitted letters with an apostrophe to suggest pronunciation, for example, 'nothin'' (Act Two, p. 64)
- phonetic spelling: spelling a word as it is pronounced, for example, 'Yeh' (Act Two, p. 76)
- contraction: merging two words together to suggest pronunciation, for example, 'y' ma' (Act One, p. 43)
- slang: very informal language choices, for example, 'bunk' (Act One, p. 43), 'poshy' (Act One, p. 31)
- dialect, for example, 'soft' (Act One, p. 31).

It is immediately noticeable that the working class characters' dialogue is written to suggest their accent and their use of dialect and slang.

> **TOP TIP** (A02)
>
> When you write about a character's use of language, you can often reinforce your point by comparing it to another character's language; for example, by comparing Mickey and Edward's language, or Mrs Johnstone's and Mrs Lyons's.

LANGUAGE DEVICE: CHARACTER AND VOICE

What is voice?	The language the writer chooses to suggest the way a character speaks
Example	'Oh, that sounds like super fun. ... You say smashing things, don't you?' (Act One, p. 28)
Effect	Edward's use of the adjectives 'super' and 'smashing' suggests his social class, his enthusiastic personality and his immediate admiration for Mickey.

Russell makes careful vocabulary choices to establish and develop character. Compare the language choices Russell uses to create the characters of Mickey and Edward as seven year olds:

> **Edward** ... Are you going to come and play up there again?
>
> **Mickey** No. I would do but I'm not allowed.
>
> **Edward** Why?
>
> **Mickey** Cos me mam says.
>
> **Edward** Well, my mummy doesn't allow me to play down here actually. (Act One, p. 27)

Both characters have a limited vocabulary and use relatively simple sentence structures, typical of a seven year old. However, Edward speaks in complete sentences while Mickey speaks in sentence fragments; Edward refers to his mother as 'mummy', while Mickey refers to his mother as 'mam'. Russell's choices suggest that Edward's speech is more formal while Mickey's is more informal, reflecting their home lives and social class.

Russell also uses characters' voices to suggest their relationship. Compare Mrs Johnstone's and Mrs Lyons's dialogue as they admire baby Edward:

> **Mrs Lyons** If he needs picking up, I shall pick him up. All right?
>
> **Mrs Johnstone** Well, I just thought, I'm sorry, I ... (Act One, p. 20)

Mrs Lyons voice is given dominant aggression using the authoritative 'shall' and the confrontational 'all right?' while Mrs Johnstone's submissive hesitation is reflected in the use of ellipsis and incomplete sentences.

In addition to the action on stage, Russell uses the Narrator to create and change the mood and atmosphere of the play:

- For example, just before Edward goes to university, the audience sees a montage of events from Mickey, Edward and Linda's teenage years. The Narrator emphasises the carefree optimism of three teenagers on the verge of adulthood: 'everything is possible, the world's within your reach' (Act Two, p. 83).

- The Narrator then signals a change of mood using the metaphor of the seasons changing to suggest that their optimism is misplaced: 'It was one day in October when the sun began to fade, / And winter broke the promise that the summer had just made' (Act Two, p. 87).

In the scene that follows, Mickey announces Linda's pregnancy and their marriage, but then learns that he has lost his job.

TOP TIP (A02)

You will not get any credit for simply pointing out the name of a language device that the writer has used. Always comment on its effect.

TOP TIP (A02)

Think about Russell's use of motifs in the play: images or ideas that recur throughout the text, suggesting their significance to the text as a whole. For example, references to Marilyn Monroe, dancing and guns are made throughout *Blood Brothers*.

AIMING HIGH: DRAMATIC INITIATIVE

When considering characters' relationships and interactions, you should consider what they say, but also how much they say and the extent to which this gives them the dramatic initiative: the extent to which they control the events in that scene. For example, look carefully at the confrontation between Mrs Lyons and Mrs Johnstone in Act Two (pp. 77–9). As Mrs Lyons first confronts Mrs Johnstone, she speaks the majority of the dialogue: her lines are full of aggressive questions while Mrs Johnstone's are full of hesitant ellipses. However, Mrs Johnstone delivers her longest speech of the scene when she refuses to accept Mrs Lyons's money, effectively taking the dramatic initiative from her. This victory is challenged as Mrs Lyons tries to attack her with a knife but is reaffirmed when Mrs Johnstone disarms her and sends her away, so regaining the dramatic initiative.

LANGUAGE DEVICE: IMAGERY

What is imagery?	Language chosen to convey an idea by creating a visual image in the reader or audience's mind
Example	The Narrator describes Mickey, Edward and Linda on the beach: 'An' you don't even notice broken bottles in the sand' (Act Two, p. 83)
Effect	The visual image created by this metaphor suggests that, while the teenagers enjoy themselves at the beach, hidden dangers lie in their path and they should be wary.

Willy Russell is a realist. His aim, in the language he gives to his characters, is to re-create the voices of real people. The Narrator, however, is placed outside the events of the play and is often given lines that make use of imagery to convey or comment on the events in the play:

- His repeated allusions to superstition are images of impending doom intended to build tension in the audience.

- His references to 'debt' (Act One, p. 16) refer literally to the debt which Mrs Johnstone owes to the Milkman and Catalogue Man, and the baby she has agreed to hand over to Mrs Lyons – but are also intended as a metaphor suggesting that she will one day pay a much greater price for entering into this agreement.

REVISION FOCUS: THE NARRATOR'S LANGUAGE

Select three of the Narrator's longer speeches, and consider how he uses imagery to direct the audience's response to the characters' actions and choices or to hint at how the plot will develop.

PROGRESS AND REVISION CHECK

SECTION ONE: CHECK YOUR KNOWLEDGE

(1) Name two elements in the play that are typical of the genre of tragedy.

(2) Identify three parallels in the lives of Mickey and Edward.

(3) How does Russell create contrast between Mrs Johnstone and Mrs Lyons? Give two examples.

(4) At a key turning point in the play, Russell combines a happy, celebratory event with a disastrous event which begins Mickey's downfall. What are the two events?

(5) Name three things that happen to Mickey after his marriage and which signal his downward spiral to a tragic death.

(6) What does the term 'dialect' mean?

(7) What does the term 'accent' mean?

(8) Give one example of how Russell represents the Liverpudlian accent in his dialogue.

(9) Which character uses the most imagery in their lines?

(10) What impact are the Narrator's repeated allusions to superstition intended to have on the audience?

TOP TIP (A01)

Answer these quick questions to test your basic knowledge of the form, structure and language of the play.

SECTION TWO: CHECK YOUR UNDERSTANDING

Task: How does Russell use the play's structure to show the changing relationship of Mickey and Edward? Think about:

● Parallels and contrasts between Mickey and Edward

● How the audience might respond to their changing relationship

TOP TIP (A01)

This task requires more thought and a slightly longer response. Try to write at least three to four paragraphs.

PROGRESS CHECK

GOOD PROGRESS

I can:

● explain how Russell uses form, structure and language to develop the action, show relationships and develop ideas. ☐

● use relevant quotations to support the points I make, and make reference to the effect of some language choices. ☐

EXCELLENT PROGRESS

I can:

● analyse in detail Russell's use of particular forms, structures and language techniques to convey ideas, create characters and evoke mood or setting. ☐

● select from a range of evidence, including apt quotations, to infer the effect of particular language choices and to develop wider interpretations. ☐

UNDERSTANDING THE QUESTION

For your exam, you will be answering a question on the whole text and/or a question on an extract from *Blood Brothers*. Check with your teacher to see what sort of question you are doing. Whatever the task, questions in exams will need **decoding**. This means highlighting and understanding the key words so the answer you write is relevant.

BREAK DOWN THE QUESTION

Pick out the **key words** or phrases. For example:

Question: How does Willy Russell **present parents and children** in *Blood Brothers?* Write about:

- Parents and children and their relationships in *Blood Brothers*
- How Russell presents these relationships by the way he writes

What does this tell you?

- Focus on the **theme of parents and children and their relationships**
- The word **'present'** tells you that you should focus on the ways Russell reveals these relationships, i.e. the techniques he uses.

PLANNING YOUR ANSWER

It is vital that you generate ideas quickly and plan your answer efficiently when you sit the exam. Stick to your plan and, with a watch at your side, tick off each part as you progress.

STAGE 1: GENERATE IDEAS QUICKLY

Briefly **list your key ideas** based on the question you have **decoded**. For example:

- *Mrs Johnstone's decision to give up one of her twins*
- *The relationship between Mrs Lyons and Edward*
- *The relationship between Mrs Johnstone and her children, Mickey in particular*

STAGE 2: JOT DOWN USEFUL QUOTATIONS (OR KEY EVENTS)

For example:

- Mrs Johnstone: 'With one more baby we could have managed. But not with two.' (Act One, p. 11)
- Mrs Lyons: 'You see, you see why I don't want you mixing with boys like that!' (Act One, p. 37)

STAGE 3: PLAN FOR PARAGRAPHS

Use paragraphs to plan your answer. For example:

Paragraph	Point
Paragraph 1	**Introduce** the **argument** you wish to make: *Russell explores the theme of parents and children through the relationships between Mrs Johnstone and her twins, and between Mrs Lyons and Edward.*
Paragraph 2	Your first point: *Mrs Johnstone is driven by her financial situation to give up one of her twins. She thinks this will give the child a better life.*
Paragraph 3	Your second point: *Despite her agreement with Mrs Lyons, Mrs Johnstone cannot reject Edward. She sends him away the first time, but later gives him a locket.*
Paragraph 4	Your third point: *Mrs Lyons tries to protect Edward from the dangers of the world and, in particular, from children like Mickey.*
Paragraph 5	Your fourth point: *Mrs Johnstone always tries to do her best for her children and allows them much more freedom than Mrs Lyons allows Edward.* (You may want to add further paragraphs if you have time.)
Conclusion	**Sum up** your argument: *By contrasting Mrs Johnstone's and Mrs Lyons's very different relationships with their children, Russell creates sympathy for Mrs Johnstone and for Edward and Mickey. All three were affected by Mrs Johnstone's poverty and the agreement she was forced to make because of it.*

TOP TIP (A01)

You may not have time to write such a detailed plan in the exam, but this is a good example of how to structure your ideas into paragraphs. Remember to back up your points with evidence from the text, events or quotations.

TOP TIP (A02)

When discussing Russell's use of language, make sure you refer to the techniques he uses and, most importantly, the *effect* of those techniques. Don't just say, 'Russell uses lots of adjectives and adverbs here'; write, 'Russell's use of adjectives and adverbs shows/demonstrates/conveys the ideas that …'.

RESPONDING TO WRITERS' EFFECTS

The two most important assessment objectives are **AO1** and **AO2** (except for Edexcel, where you will only be examined on AO1, AO3 and AO4). They are about *what* writers do (the choices they make, and the effects these create), *what* your ideas are (your analysis and interpretation) and *how* you write about them (how well you explain your ideas).

ASSESSMENT OBJECTIVE 1

What does it say?	What does it mean?	Dos and don'ts
Read, understand and respond to texts. Students should be able to: ● Maintain a critical style and develop an informed personal response ● Use textual references, including quotations, to support and illustrate interpretations	You must: ● Use some of the literary terms you have learned (correctly!) ● Write in a professional way (not a sloppy, chatty way) ● Show that you have thought for yourself ● Back up your ideas with examples, including quotations	**Don't write …** *Mickey is really poor and Russell makes him speak really bad English to show he is working class.* **Do write …** *Russell uses abbreviation and phonetic spelling to create Mickey's Liverpudlian accent. He tells Edward to 'Gis a sweet' when they first meet. Russell suggests the class difference between them when Mickey teaches Edward to swear which Edward, using middle class vocabulary, describes as 'smashing'.*

IMPROVING YOUR CRITICAL STYLE

Use a variety of words and phrases to show effects:

> **Russell** *suggests …, conveys …, implies …, presents how …, explores …, demonstrates …, shows how …*
> **The audience** *infer …, recognise …, understand …, question …, see …, are given …, reflect …*

For example, look at these two alternative paragraphs by different students about Mickey. Note the difference in the quality of expression.

Student A:

Vague

Repeats the point from the beginning of the paragraph – better to develop it

Willy Russell shows that Mickey is really rough all the time. He says he wants to urinate through people's letter boxes and he thinks Sammy is impressive because he can spit in people's eyes. This shows that Mickey does not really care about other people. This shows that he is rough. Russell is showing that Mickey is just a child but is also entertaining for the audience.

Chatty and informal

Unclear whether 'He' refers to Russell or Mickey

Repetitive – better to use an alternative

Student B:

Appropriate language choice to comment on the ways in which Mickey is shown	Russell presents Mickey as a mischievous boy who admires his older brother's antisocial behaviour when he first appears on stage, aged seven. Russell emphasises his frustration at being treated like a seven year old when he's 'nearly eight' with constant repetition of the phrase as the refrain to his song. Russell introduces Mickey as a naughty but endearingly entertaining boy, typical of all seven year olds.	Clear and precise language
Clear and precise language		Good variety of vocabulary
Focuses on the audience's likely response		Focus on language choice
		Looks beyond the obvious with personal interpretation

ASSESSMENT OBJECTIVE 2   (A02)

What does it say?	What does it mean?	Dos and don'ts
Analyse the language, form and structure used by the writer to create meanings and effects, using relevant subject terminology where appropriate.	'Analyse' – comment **in detail** on **particular aspects** of the text or language. 'Language' – vocabulary, imagery, variety of sentences, dialogue/speech, etc. 'Form' – **how** the story is told (e.g. dialogue, song, the role of the Narrator) 'Structure' – the **order** in which events are revealed, or in which characters appear 'create meanings' – what can we, as an audience, **infer** from the characters and their dialogue? What is **implied** by particular speeches, or events? 'Subject terminology' – **words** you should use when writing about plays, such as 'character', 'imagery', 'setting', etc.	**Don't write …** *The Narrator tells you what happens in the play so you can understand the story.* **Do write …** *Russell uses the Narrator to explain the story, but more importantly to create tension as he never allows the audience to forget the play's ending which he revealed at its beginning. He makes constant allusions to superstition and to the devil 'starin' through your windows' to emphasise that every action and decision the characters take will eventually have devastating consequences.*

IMPLICATIONS, INFERENCES AND INTERPRETATIONS

- The best analysis focuses on specific ideas or events, or uses of language and thinks about what is **implied**.

- This means drawing **inferences**. On the surface, Mickey and Edward's games at the age of seven are depicted as harmless fun, but what deeper ideas do they suggest and foreshadow about Mickey's attitude to guns and to figures of authority such as the Policeman, and about the relationship between Mickey and Edward?

- From the inferences you make across the text as a whole, you can arrive at your own **interpretation** – a sense of the bigger picture, a wider evaluation of a character, relationship or idea.

USING QUOTATIONS

One of the secrets of success in writing exam essays is to use quotations **effectively**. There are five basic principles:

1. Only quote what is most useful.
2. Do not use a quotation that repeats what you have just written.
3. Put quotation marks, e.g. ' ', around the quotation.
4. Write the quotation exactly as it appears in the original.
5. Use the quotation so that it fits neatly into your sentence.

EXAM FOCUS: USING QUOTATIONS (A01)

Quotations should be used to develop the line of thought in your essay, and to 'zoom in' on key details, such as language choices. The **mid-level example** below shows a clear and effective way of doing this:

Makes a clear point

At first, Russell presents Mrs Lyons as unhappy because she cannot have children. She says that 'We've been trying for such a long time now'. Russell makes her a sympathetic character that the audience can feel sorry for because she is so disappointed.

Gives an apt quotation

Explains the effect of the quotation

However, really **high-level responses** will go further. They will make an even more precise point, support it with an even more appropriate quotation, focus in on particular words and phrases, and explain the effect or what is implied to make a wider point or draw inferences. Here is an example:

Precise point

At first, Russell presents Mrs Lyons as a sympathetic figure, suffering from loneliness and unfulfilled dreams. She explains to Mrs Johnstone that 'we bought such a large house for the – for the children – we thought children would come along' The use of dashes and repetition conveys to the audience her hesitation and discomfort, suggesting her sadness and perhaps her reluctance to talk so openly to Mrs Johnstone. By creating this sympathy, Russell justifies Mrs Johnstone's decision to give away one of her twins, but also increases the audience's shock when Mrs Lyons dramatically changes once she's been given the baby she so desperately wants.

Precise quotation

Language feature

Explanation/ implication/effect

Further development/link

SPELLING, PUNCTUATION AND GRAMMAR

SPELLING

Remember to spell correctly the **playwright's** name, the names of all the **characters**, and the names of **places**.

Before your exam, learn to spell the key literature terms you might use when writing about the text such as: ironic, tragedy, resolution, scene, character, theme, audience, etc.

PUNCTUATION

Remember:

- Use **full stops and commas in sentences accurately to make clear points**. Don't write long, rambling sentences that don't make sense; equally, avoid using a lot of short repetitive ones. Write in a fluent way, using linking words and phrases, and use **inverted commas** for **quotations**:

Don't write	Do write
Mickey and Edward have a very strong relationship from the moment they meet at the age of seven as they talk and play together and Mickey teaches Edward about swear words even though he does not really know what they mean and is not as tough and streetwise as he pretends to be.	*Throughout their teenage years, Edward encourages Mickey to express his feelings to Linda while hiding his own. His unselfish friendship creates enormous sympathy in the audience, but it creates an even greater shock when he and Linda start an affair near the end of the play.*

GRAMMAR

When you are writing about the text, make sure you:

- Use the present tense for discussing what the writer does, e.g. *Russell shows how poverty and desperation can drive people to make extreme choices.*
- Vary character names with pronouns (he/her) and use references back to make your writing flow.

Don't write	Do write
Russell showed the bond between Mrs Johnstone and Edward when Mrs Johnstone gave Edward a locket containing a picture of Mrs Johnstone and Mickey which Edward wore constantly.	*Russell shows the bond between Mrs Johnstone and Edward when **she** gives **him** a locket containing a picture of **her** and Mickey which **he** wears constantly.*

TOP TIP A04

Remember that spelling, punctuation and grammar may be worth **around 5 per cent** of your overall mark. You should always aim to make your writing as accurate and fluent as possible, to get your points across to the examiner.

TOP TIP A04

Enliven your essay by varying the way your sentences begin. For example, *Russell dramatically undermines the joy of Mickey's wedding by contrasting it with Mr Lyons singing cheerfully about making his workers redundant,* can also be written as: *By contrasting it with Mr Lyons singing cheerfully about making his workers redundant, Russell dramatically undermines the joy of Mickey's wedding.*

ANNOTATED SAMPLE ANSWERS

This section will provide you with three **sample responses**, one at a **mid** level, one at a **good** level, and one at a **very high** level. This is an AQA style question which assesses all four AOs. However, it will also be useful for checking your own level if you are following the Eduqas or Edexcel specifications.

> How does Willy Russell present ideas about friendship in the play? Write about:
>
> ● How the nature of friendship changes due to circumstances or time
> ● How Russell explores these ideas through the way he writes

SAMPLE ANSWER 1

A01 Introduces the main basic idea of friendship in the play

Willy Russell presents friendship as a very important idea in the play and as an important part of two of the main characters' lives. Mickey and Edward are best friends from the age of seven until they are eighteen when it all goes wrong.

A01 New point signalled in new paragraph

A02 An explanation, but expressed rather clumsily and does not highlight the literary device used (irony)

Mickey and Edward meet for the first time when they are seven years old in Act One. They become good friends straight away and decide to become blood brothers when they find out they have the same birthday. Mickey says Edward is his 'best friend' and they have lots of things in common, like they both enjoy swearing and playing with guns which shows how similar they are but they don't realise that they are actually real brothers even though the audience knows.

A01 Informal expression unsuitable – should use a critical style

A02 A clear, detailed explanation

However, Edward and Mickey are very different because their mum gave Edward away and now he thinks Mrs Lyons is his mum. Edward is very impressed with Mickey because he knows some swear words. Edward says he will look it up in the dictionary but Mickey does not know what a dictionary is. This shows that Edward comes from an educated family background but Mickey comes from a poorer background where he has learned swear words at a very young age.

Russell shows how similar and how different the two twins are for most of the play. For example, they both get suspended from their schools when they are fourteen for refusing to cooperate with their teachers. These two things happen separately but are shown at exactly the same time in the play which suggests that there are some very strong connections between the lives of Mickey and Edward. However, there is a

A03 Reference to the context in which the play is set

very great difference between their backgrounds. Mickey goes to a secondary modern which was a school that less intelligent children had to go to if they were not clever enough to get into grammar school. This shows that Mickey was not very good at schoolwork. Edward on the other hand goes to a private boarding school which shows how much money Mr and Mrs Lyons have got and how different they are to Mrs Johnstone.

A03 Understanding of context

Russell really shows how big these differences are when the twins get to the age of eighteen. Edward goes off to university and Mickey gets a job making cardboard boxes in a factory. This shows the different kinds of futures and opportunities that the rich and poor had when the play was written and how much it affects their lives. When Edward comes back from university he can't understand why Mickey is so upset about having no money. Mickey says Edward is 'still a kid' because he can't understand: 'beat it before I hit y', and that's pretty much the last time they speak to each other until right at the end of the play. It shows how being an adult changes everything and can end friendships.

A01 A relevant quotation but not fully embedded or explained

A01 Informal expression unsuitable – should use a critical style

A04 Sentence too long – there are several sentences contained in one; also includes irrelevant details

After that Edward has an affair with Linda when Mickey won't give up his anti-depressant pills after he comes out of prison and he gets him a new job and a new house but Mickey knows how that happened and is really angry with Linda for arranging it. This shows that Edward is really selfish and not Mickey's friend anymore because that's not how friends should behave. When he finds out about the affair, Mickey shoots Edward which is really sad because they were once such great and inseparable friends but Mickey's life and all the bad things that have happened to him have driven them apart.

A01 Needs to draw together the main points or find an interesting way to sum up

MID LEVEL

Comment

An understanding of the theme is expressed and some sound points are made. Paragraphs are used effectively, but vocabulary is limited and words or expressions repeated. The overall effect is too chatty in tone. The student needs to write in a more formal style and should also discuss the effects Russell creates, referring to literary devices.

For a Good Level:

- Develop a formal critical style, drawing on a wider range of vocabulary, and avoid informal language or slang.
- Use literary devices and show how the playwright creates effects from the language he chooses.
- Make sure quotations are embedded in sentences so that when a sentence is read it flows.

SAMPLE ANSWER 2

A01 — Clear introduction that outlines the essential points

Russell puts Mickey and Edward's friendship at the centre of the play, 'Blood Brothers'. The breakdown of that friendship leads to the ending which the play builds up to from the moment the Narrator reveals it in the opening scene.

Mickey and Edward become friends within minutes of their first meeting. They decide that, because they share a birthday, they will seal their friendship by becoming blood brothers. Neither of them realises that they are in fact twins, separated at birth. Mickey is even prepared to stand up to his older brother Sammy when he calls Edward a 'poshy'. Mickey says that Edward is his 'best friend', showing that he is prepared to stand up to his impressive, intimidating big brother for this friendship.

A01 — Quotations are embedded fluently in sentences

Russell shows huge differences between the twins because of their very different upbringings. Mickey swears freely, which Edward thinks is 'smashing'. The adjective 'smashing', and Edward's plan to look up the swear word in the dictionary, strongly suggest that Edward comes from a middle class, educated background very different from Mickey's. However, their differences are irrelevant to the two best friends.

A02 — Explains the combined effect of a quote and textual reference

Mickey and Edward continue to be best friends in their teenage years with many parallels in their lives. For example, both of them are suspended from their very different schools when they challenge the authority of their teachers. This shows again that, although they are different, they have very similar attitudes and personalities, reminding the audience that they are not just friends, but really are blood brothers.

A04 — Shifts successfully to a new paragraph

One thing they have in common is their love of Linda. Mickey is too shy to tell her and Edward hides his feelings because of his friendship with Mickey. This is ironic because after the breakdown of their friendship near the end of Act Two, it is Edward's affair with Linda which drives Mickey to shoot Edward dead by mistake.

A02 — Highlights a literary device and shows its relevance

A01 — Informal expression – should use more precise, critical style

Mickey and Edward's friendship cannot stand the pressures of adulthood. As they turn eighteen, Russell highlights how they are drifting apart because of their different backgrounds. Edward goes to university while Mickey gets a job in a factory.

A02 Explains the effect by highlighting the key word

When Edward returns from university, he finds that Mickey is married to Linda, who is pregnant, and that Mickey has been made redundant. They argue because Edward cannot understand the pressures that Mickey is under. Mickey calls him a 'kid' who hasn't grown up because he 'didn't need to'. The word 'kid' suggests that Edward has not changed since the beginning of the play. He has a good life and does not really understand what is happening in Mickey's life.

A03 Reference to context but needs to be linked to author's purpose

After this point in the play there is very little dialogue between Edward and Mickey, showing how far apart their lives have drifted and how damaged their friendship is. Edward becomes a councillor, while Mickey loses his job, commits a crime, is sent to prison and becomes hooked on anti-depressants. This was a problem in the early eighties when the play was written. However Russell also highlights the damage it does to friendship and to family. It leads to Mickey's final confrontation with Edward when they discover their true relationship.

A01 Informal expression – should use more precise, critical style

A01 Reference to the rest of the play

A02 A sound conclusion

The twins' friendship and brotherhood cannot save their lives at the end of the play. Russell builds up their friendship for most of the play, creating a heart-warming story of two very different people's bond of friendship. When their social class and circumstances drive that friendship apart, it is all the more tragic.

GOOD LEVEL

Comment
This is a confident response to the question and demonstrates a good understanding of the theme and how it is presented. The context of the play has also been mentioned. Literary devices have been highlighted and there is some exploration of language to emphasise effects. Quotations are relevant and fluently embedded in sentences, but occasionally the language is a little informal.

For a High Level:
- Refer more to Russell's control of language and purpose.
- Link context references to the author's purpose.
- Extend the range of vocabulary, and look for more sophisticated words to express ideas.
- Be careful not to use informal language, but to develop a critical style.
- Use long and short sentences to vary pace, and alter sentence openers for variety.

SAMPLE ANSWER 3

AO1 Excellent opening that presents the relevance of the theme in the text

Friendship, and the breakdown of friendship, are at the heart of the tragedy of 'Blood Brothers'. Russell uses that tragedy to highlight issues of poverty and crime and their impact on real people, which he considered was the direct result of government policy in the early 1980s when the play was written.

AO3 Follows on using a literary term to state the author's purpose, linking the text with the context in which it was written

Fate seems to play a significant part in the friendship of Mickey and Edward. Despite being separated at birth, and the best efforts of Mrs Johnstone and Mrs Lyons, they meet at the age of seven and, ironically, become best friends and blood brothers almost immediately. Russell seems to be suggesting that their shared and inevitable fate will not allow them to be separated — or perhaps their similar interests in swearing and sweets implies brotherhood. It is, though, essential to the play's structure that the brothers are drawn to each other: the drama relies on their friendship.

AO2 Awareness of a range of interpretations, of structure and the writer's craft

AO4 Precise, well-chosen vocabulary to describe the writer's craft

Russell manufactures coincidences in the twins' lives: both families move from Liverpool to Skelmersdale; both boys are suspended from school; they meet again accidentally aged fourteen. When they meet, each eyes the other jealously from a distance. Crippled by a lack of confidence in their appearance, each wishes they could be 'a little less like me' and more 'like that guy'. Ironically, of course, being twins, they are exactly like 'that guy'.

AO2 Quotations clearly embedded in the text with interpretation of language device and effect

AO1 Highly effective synthesis of textual reference

There are, however, significant differences between Mickey and Edward which eventually drive them apart. In childhood, neither seems aware of any difference in their social class. Sammy calls Edward a 'poshy', suggesting that he and Mickey cannot possibly be friends. Mickey immediately denies it, declaring that Edward is his 'best friend', even though Russell has made clear to the audience that Edward is very much a 'poshy', speaking in standard English, living in a large house in the park, consulting the dictionary. Edward is sent to a private boarding school while Mickey goes to the local secondary modern school. Neither of the twins comments or otherwise reflects on the vast difference in opportunity, privilege or class which this represents.

It is in adulthood that this difference drives the twins apart. When Edward returns from university he finds that Mickey has married Linda, is expecting a baby and has lost his job. While Mickey feels the pressure of his responsibilities, Edward

A02 Precise comment on language choice and detailed analysis of effect

A02 Precise focus on language choice

A04 Sharp, effective use of language to reinforce the point

cannot understand them. He asks Mickey 'why is a job so important?'. Russell frames this as a question, not a statement, revealing a great deal about Edward: he has no awareness of the privilege which Mr Lyons's job has allowed him or the problems which poverty brings. Mickey's response is blunt. He dismisses Edward as 'still a kid' and their friendship as 'just kids' stuff', the adverb 'just' emphasising how little he thinks of it now.

From this point, the opportunities of privilege and the consequences of class become more apparent as the twins progress to their inevitable deaths. Edward returns to the parties of university; Mickey robs a filling station and is sent to prison. Edward becomes a local councillor; Mickey is released from prison addicted to anti-depressants. Whereas once Mickey was happy to take 'sweets an' ciggies' from Edward, he is too proud to accept a new job and a new house from him. This is not simply because 'a job and a house' are a more valuable favour. It is because Mickey is now aware of the differences between himself and Edward and he resents them.

A01 Quotations clearly embedded in the text with interpretation of their significance

A01 Excellent conclusion exploring an original and perceptive interpretation

Mickey's resentment builds when he learns that Edward has taken the 'one thing left in my life': Linda. However it is Mrs Johnstone's revelation that they are twins which finally drives Mickey's resentment to its peak: 'I could have been him!' Despite this jealousy of Edward, and the shooting that follows, Mickey tells Edward, 'I was gonna shoot y'. But I can't even do that.' In the end, Mickey has no intention of shooting his brother: the gun goes off accidentally. Despite the tragedy of the twins' death, and the devastating impact of social class on their friendship, Russell cannot apparently bring himself to end the twins' relationship in the absolute tragedy of an intentional killing. He leaves the audience some small hope and faith in friendship and brotherhood at the end of the play.

VERY HIGH LEVEL

Comment
This is an excellent analysis of the theme of friendship. There is good understanding of literary techniques, and sound analysis of language and its effect. Links have been made to other features of the play, particularly to the central theme of class and also to the playwright's main purpose. A sophisticated range of vocabulary has been used and the sentence structure has pace and variety. The conclusion presents an unusual and well-supported argument about the play's resolution.

PRACTICE TASK

Write a full-length response to this exam-style question and then use the **Mark scheme** on page 88 to assess your own response.

> How does Willy Russell present ideas about social class in the play?
>
> Write about:
>
> - The impact of social class on the characters and their lives in the play
> - How Russell explores these ideas through the way he writes

TOP TIP

You can use the General skills section of the **Mark scheme** on page 88 to remind you of the key criteria you'll need to cover.

Remember:

- Plan quickly and efficiently by using key words from the question.
- Write equally about the extract and the rest of the play.
- Focus on the techniques Russell uses and the effect of these on the audience.
- Support your ideas with relevant evidence, including quotations.

FURTHER QUESTIONS

1 How does Willy Russell present superstition in *Blood Brothers*? Write about:

- The importance of superstition to the characters and the plot
- How Russell presents superstition by the ways he writes

2 **Mrs Johnstone** *I've spent all me ... life knowin' I* shouldn't. *But I do.*

Explore the role of Mrs Johnstone in *Blood Brothers*.

You **must** refer to the context of the play in your answer.

3 **a)** Read the extract from page 61 (from *On the other side of the stage, Mrs Lyons...* to *He exits*). Look at how Edward and Mrs Lyons speak and behave here. What does it reveal about their characters and their relationship at this point in the play? Refer closely to details from the extract to support your answer.

b) Write about the relationship between parents and children and how they are presented at different points in the play.

LITERARY TERMS

accent	a particular way of pronouncing words which can reveal where the speaker is from
allusion	an indirect reference to something, e.g. another text
ambiguity	doubt or uncertainty of meaning
atmosphere	a setting's or situation's mood
dialect	vocabulary and/or grammar which is specific to a particular group, area or region
dialogue	the words that are spoken by characters in conversation
dramatic device	a trick or technique used by the playwright to create emotional impact or influence the action, such as dramatic irony
dramatic initiative	taking control of the events on stage and of the audience's attention
ellipsis	a punctuation mark of three dots (...) suggesting an incomplete sentence or pause
foreshadow	when a writer hints at what is to come
genre	a type of literature, for instance, poetry, drama, biography, fiction; or style of literature, for example, Gothic or romance
imagery	creating a word picture; common forms are metaphors and similes
irony	saying one thing while meaning another, often through understatement, concealment or indirect statement. Dramatic irony is when the audience or reader is aware of something but the character in the play is not
juxtaposition	two ideas, images or objects positioned close together to highlight their differences
metaphor	a figure of speech in which something, someone or an action is described as something else in order to imply a resemblance, e.g. 'broken bottles in the sand' (Act Two, p. 83) is a metaphor for the problems that Mickey, Edward and Linda will soon encounter
montage	a series of images or very short scenes, often used to suggest a sequence of events taking place over a period of time
motif	an image, idea or situation which recurs throughout the text, forming a pattern, e.g. guns, dancing, Marilyn Monroe
narrator	the voice telling the story or relating a sequence of events
omniscient narrator	a narrator with God-like knowledge of the world of the story. They can see all the characters' thoughts and actions and can tell the story from different viewpoints
plot device	a feature of a text used to manipulate its plot
realist	a writer who depicts ordinary life in a down-to-earth way
resolution	the conclusion or ending of a story
setting	the place or environment where the events in a story are set. Settings are sometimes used to create a mood, reflect a character's inner feelings, or are used symbolically
slang	very informal language, used by a particular group of people
soliloquy	when a character speaks directly to the audience as if thinking aloud, revealing their inner thoughts, feelings and intentions
stage directions	the part of a playscript that gives directions about scenery or setting, or suggests how the actors should move or speak their lines
standard English	the dialect of English that is used in formal speech and writing
stereotype	a common and oversimplified idea of what a particular type of person or thing is like
symbolise	to use an image to mean or represent something else, often an idea or emotion

CHECKPOINT ANSWERS

CHECKPOINT 1, page 9

Mickey and Edward's lives seem most similar when they are young, most different when they are adults.

CHECKPOINT 2, PAGE 10

Milk is a basic necessity – particularly when pregnant. The fact she is struggling to pay for it highlights the difficulties Mrs Johnstone is facing.

CHECKPOINT 3, PAGE 12

He would always have food and decent clothing, toys and a garden to play in, etc.

CHECKPOINT 4, PAGE 15

Through the Narrator, Russell suggests that Mrs Johnstone is creating another debt in giving her child away – and that the debt will have to be repaid, i.e. there will be consequences.

CHECKPOINT 5, PAGE 18

They have very quickly become friends and they share a birthday.

CHECKPOINT 6, PAGE 20

In the previous section (Act One, p. 31), Mickey and Sammy were playing with toy guns. This suggests that, though very different in some ways, Mickey and Edward are both typical children.

CHECKPOINT 7, PAGE 21

An audience might react with shock or amusement.

CHECKPOINT 8, PAGE 24

It could suggest that little will change.

CHECKPOINT 9, PAGE 26

She blames the teacher for letting the students play with magnesium.

CHECKPOINT 10, PAGE 32

She says she would spend it on 'junk and trash' – she also does not want to accept Mrs Lyons's bribe to make her move house as she has 'made a life out here' (Act Two, p. 78).

CHECKPOINT 11, PAGE 33

Mickey has a job; Edward is going to university.

CHECKPOINT 12, PAGE 34

The move into October and from summer to winter reflects a change in mood: from the happiness of the twins' teenage years to the difficulties they will face as adults.

CHECKPOINT 13, PAGE 39

The only evidence Mickey gives for this conclusion is that Linda and Edward were friends when she got pregnant.

PROGRESS AND REVISION CHECK ANSWERS

PART TWO, page 40

SECTION ONE: CHECK YOUR KNOWLEDGE

1. Mickey and Edward's deaths
2. The Milkman complains that he has not been paid.
3. Nine
4. Mr Lyons needs to be away so that Mrs Lyons can tell him she was pregnant and that Edward is their birth child.
5. She tells them the other twin has gone to heaven.
6. Fifty pounds
7. A sweet
8. Edward tells Mrs Lyons that he likes Mickey more than her and swears at her.
9. He tells Mrs Johnstone that she will end up in court; he suggests Mrs Lyons docks Edward's pocket money and keeps him away from people like Mickey.
10. A toy gun
11. He goes to a single-sex boarding school.
12. A photograph of Mickey and Mrs Johnstone
13. Mrs Lyons thinks the photo is of Edward and Mrs Johnstone, because Mickey and Edward are twins and so look very similar.
14. She thinks Mrs Johnstone is following her and thinks it may be the only way to stop her from doing so.
15. He is telling Linda that he has always loved her.
16. Linda has asked Edward, now a local councillor, to help him.
17. Mickey gets the gun from under a floorboard where Sammy hid it after the filling station robbery.
18. Mrs Lyons points it out to him.
19. The police
20. Superstition and class

SECTION TWO: CHECK YOUR UNDERSTANDING

Task 1

- It shows how desperate Mrs Lyons is to make Edward her own.
- It reveals Mrs Lyons's heartlessness as she knows how reliant Mrs Johnstone is on her wages.
- It encourages the audience's sympathy for Mrs Johnstone and antipathy to Mrs Lyons.
- Mrs Lyons is attempting to sever any connection between Mrs Johnstone's family and Edward. The remainder of the play explores the consequences of that apparently unbreakable connection.

Task 2

- The sequence shows the final summer that the three friends spend together as teenagers.
- After this sequence, Mickey and Linda finally become a couple: a traditional happy ending.

- In sharp contrast, this sequence is followed by pregnancy, marriage, redundancy, crime, prison, addiction and death. This sequence is therefore part of a highly significant transition from childhood to adulthood.
- The Narrator warns the audience that the three friends are oblivious to the inevitable consequences which will follow.

PART THREE, page 52

SECTION ONE: CHECK YOUR KNOWLEDGE

1. She wants him to have something of hers which will remind him of her and Mickey.

2. One of the things that Edward admires about Mickey is that he knows lots of swear words.

3. Edward persuades Mickey to tell Linda how he feels about her.

4. Edward swears at Mrs Lyons.

5. Sammy burns down his school, threatens a bus conductor and shoots someone while attempting to rob a filling station.

6. Linda supports Mickey on the bus, when they are suspended, and when Mickey is taking anti-depressants.

7. At the start of the play Russell shows her disappointment at being unable to have children.

8. He suggests she goes to see a doctor.

9. The Milkman and the Gynaecologist are the only two additional roles that the script allocates to the Narrator, however the director may choose to allocate him additional roles, for example, that of the Judge or the Policeman.

10. The teachers speak aggressively to the twins and they suspend them for relatively minor misdemeanours.

SECTION TWO: CHECK YOUR UNDERSTANDING

- Russell presents her as an affectionate and loving mother trying to do her best for her children. She gives Edward away because she is desperate and thinks it will give him a better life.
- She seems easily manipulated when Mrs Lyons persuades her to give Edward up, but appears strong and determined when Mrs Lyons threatens her with a knife.
- Her weakness is that she knows what she shouldn't do, but does it anyway – which, Russell suggests, is one reason why she never has any money.
- She allows Mickey and Edward to watch an adult film, perhaps suggesting she is broad-minded and accepting, or perhaps suggesting she is irresponsible.

PART FOUR, page 62

SECTION ONE: CHECK YOUR KNOWLEDGE

1. Boarding school, university, money

2. The friendship starts to deteriorate at Christmas when Edward comes back from university.

3. At first Mrs Lyons laughs at Mrs Johnstone's superstition but she comes to be superstitious herself.

4. For example: strict and controlling, loving but irresponsible

5 Class

6 Poverty, crime, drug abuse

7 Marilyn Monroe was a glamorous Hollywood film star who died of a drugs overdose in 1963.

8 Liverpool and Skelmersdale, 1950s to 1980s

9 He climbs on a cow.

10 The Lyons's house is in the park.

SECTION TWO: CHECK YOUR UNDERSTANDING

- Their lives are very different in terms of housing, wealth and education.
- This becomes very apparent in the twins' adult lives as Mickey goes to prison and Edward to university.
- Russell explores the impact that differences in class and wealth have on the opportunities that Mickey and Edward have in life.
- Russell uses the differences between the twins to create dramatic conflict, for example when Edward returns from university and cannot understand Mickey's problems.

PART FIVE, page 69

SECTION ONE: CHECK YOUR KNOWLEDGE

1 For example: central characters die, errors of judgement and circumstances contribute to their death.

2 For example: both are suspended, both love Linda, both die.

3 For example: Mrs Johnstone is poor and finds it difficult to control herself; Mrs Lyons is wealthy and manipulative.

4 Mickey's wedding and his redundancy

5 For example: he loses his job, goes to prison, becomes addicted to anti-depressants.

6 Dialect is the vocabulary and/ or grammar that is specific

to a particular group, area or region, for example, the Liverpudlian dialect is spoken by some people in Liverpool.

7 Accent refers to the way in which people from a specific region pronounce words.

8 The Liverpudlian accent is represented by abbreviations, for example, 'An' y' know what?' (Act One, p. 28), and phonetic spelling, for example, 'Gis a sweet' (Act One, p. 27).

9 The Narrator

10 They constantly remind the audience of the inevitable ending that awaits Mickey and Edward and so build tension.

SECTION TWO: CHECK YOUR UNDERSTANDING

- In their childhoods and teenage years Mickey and Edward are very similar, for example, playing with guns, being suspended.
- Their language and their home lives are very different.
- They fall out in adulthood as the reality of the opportunities available to them becomes clear.
- Having enjoyed the closeness of their relationship, particularly in the face of Mrs Lyons's manipulations, the breakdown of their relationship is all the more distressing for the audience.

MARK SCHEME

POINTS YOU COULD HAVE MADE

- Mrs Johnstone is forced to give away one twin because of her financial situation.
- Clear contrast with Mrs Lyons: her large house, her husband's job, the ready availability of cash.
- Despite Mrs Lyons's antagonism, Mickey and Edward's relationship seems unbreakable in childhood.
- Mickey and Edward's differences become much more apparent and significant in adulthood. They argue when Edward returns from university.

- Their differences grow as their opportunities, or lack of opportunities, allow Edward to succeed and leave Mickey struggling.
- After repeated references to the superstition that Mrs Lyons used to frighten Mrs Johnstone into silence, the Narrator suggests 'class' may be responsible for what has happened in the play.

GENERAL SKILLS

Make a judgement about your level based on the points you made (above) and the skills you showed.

Level	Key elements	Spelling, punctuation and grammar	Tick your level
Very high	**Very well-structured answer which gives a rounded and convincing viewpoint.** You use very detailed analysis of the writer's methods and effects on the reader, using precise references which are fluently woven into what you say. You draw inferences, consider more than one perspective or angle, including the context where relevant, and make interpretations about the text as a whole.	You spell and punctuate with consistent accuracy, and use a very wide range of vocabulary and sentence structures to achieve effective control of meaning.	
Good to High	**A thoughtful, detailed response with well-chosen references.** At the top end, you address all aspects of the task in a clearly expressed way, and examine key aspects in detail. You are beginning to consider implications, explore alternative interpretations or ideas; at the top end, you do this fairly regularly and with some confidence.	You spell and punctuate with considerable accuracy, and use a considerable range of vocabulary and sentence structures to achieve general control of meaning.	
Mid	**A consistent response with clear understanding of the main ideas shown.** You use a range of references to support your ideas and your viewpoint is logical and easy to follow. Some evidence of commenting on writers' effects, though more needed.	You spell and punctuate with reasonable accuracy, and use a reasonable range of vocabulary and sentence structures.	
Lower	**Some relevant ideas but an inconsistent and rather simple response in places.** You show you have understood the task and you make some points to support what you say, but the evidence is not always well chosen. Your analysis is a bit basic and you do not comment in much detail on the writer's methods.	Your spelling and punctuation is inconsistent and your vocabulary and sentence structures are both limited. Some of these make your meaning unclear.	